P9-DGU-341

Leadership in Multicultural Congregations

EMBRACING DIVERSITY

Charles R. Foster

An Alban Institute Publication

Copyright © 1997 by The Alban Institute, Inc. All rights reserved.

This material may not be photocopied or reproduced in any way without written permission.

Library of Congress Catalog Number 96-80121
ISBN 1-56699-181-1

To congregations
that challenge conventions of homogeneity
to live into the Pentecost vision
of multicultural and interracial solidarity
praising the God
who created and redeems us all

TABLE OF CONTENTS

92122

ACKNOWLEDGMENTS

Although I take full responsibility for the content of this book, many colleagues have guided me into ever deeper encounters with the diversity in God's creation. They encouraged me when I faltered, taught me in my ignorance, and gently chided me when my own racism and ethnocentrism hindered my seeing, hearing, and learning—especially Grant Shockley, Ethel Johnson, James Thomas, Jack Seymour, David Ng, Mary Elizabeth Moore, Virgil Elizondo, Joseph Crockett, Lynne Westfield, Fred Smith, Rebecca Chopp, Lorine Tevi, Ted Brelsford, and Joyce Mercer.

This project would not have happened without the financial support of Lilly Endowment, Inc., and the personal encouragement of Craig Dykstra and James P. Wind (now president of The Alban Institute) whose imaginative leadership pushes the boundaries of the consciousness of church and civic leaders. I am indebted to all the congregations whose stories of engaging cultural and racial differences in and through their ministries have inspired and chastened me. I am especially grateful to the pastors and laity of Cedar Grove United Methodist Church, Oakhurst Presbyterian Church, and Northwoods United Methodist Church in Atlanta, Georgia, for allowing a research team to spend a year with them. I am sure that our perspectives and agenda as researchers simply added to the challenges each faced in negotiating the differences already experienced among themselves.

Many other people have been resources to this project or have provided encouragement. Students in my seminary class on the Dynamics of Difference and in my doctoral seminar on the Politics of Knowing have been thoughtful teachers and insightful critics. Mary Okai and Leigh Precise have been faithful colleagues in the quest to be responsive teachers to the children of Northwoods United Methodist Church. Jerome Hamm, Nibs Stroupe, Caroline Leach, Ted Brelsford, Brian Mahan, Fred Smith, and Lorine Tevi have read and given me insightful critiques of the manuscript. Brenda Stevenson has helped ready the manuscript for publication and kept some order in the mayhem of my schedule while I have worked on it. Barbara Day and Bill Miller gave me a quiet place to work at a critical moment in the writing process.

Janet T. Foster has been my companion in the quest that has culminated in this book. I am grateful for her willingness to engage the issues that dominate my imagination, and for her steadfast love, support, encouragement.

And for Celia Allison Hahn's editorial vision for this book and the patience she and The Alban Institute staff have had with my struggles to get it written, I am grateful.

INTRODUCTION

Purpose

This book has been written for two groups of leaders in the church: (1) pastors and lay leaders of racially and culturally diverse congregations and (2) pastors, lay leaders, denominational officers, and seminary students committed to equipping the congregations they serve for living hospitably in a racially and culturally diverse society and world. It grows out of research I have done with colleagues in three *multicultural* congregations and observations from visits in many more.

The book has three purposes: (1) to explore the impact of cultural and racial diversity in U.S. and Canadian society on the identity and mission of congregations; (2) to engage readers in an examination of the dynamics of leadership in congregations that embrace racial and cultural diversity; and (3) to invite readers to explore the dynamics of "difference" at work in the leadership of their own congregations.

These three purposes shape the structure and flow of the text. Stories of leadership issues and practices in culturally and racially diverse congregations provide the framework for my discussion of congregational life and leadership. Through these stories I identify and explore patterns of congregational communication, interaction, and organization responsive to the presence of racial and cultural differences. Into the flow of these stories and interpretations I interject questions for further study and discussion, exercises to assess the extent to which a pattern or practice is present in a congregation, and guidelines for working toward the embracing of difference in some aspect of congregational life. I hope the stories I tell will help you recall similar stories from your own experience. I hope the discussion questions and exercises will provide an opportunity for you to dialogue with my interpretations of the experience of leadership in culturally and racially diverse congregations and to make decisions for strengthening the leadership in your congregations. And I hope you have as much fun reading about and working with these issues as I have had in writing about them.

Background

For readers who have not read *We Are the Church Together,* which Theodore Brelsford and I wrote after the study of three multicultural congregations,[1] a few words about me and that work may provide a useful lens through which to read this book. I am a white Anglo Saxon Protestant male. Although I have lived in most sections of the United States, I continue to identify myself with the land and regional culture of my original environs: the Pacific Northwest. Over the years I have gradually recognized the extent to which these factors associate me with dominating and oppressing structures in the church, in education, in the nation's economic and political life. And yet I have also come to believe—often reluctantly—that I have been called to engage issues of race and culture in and through my ministry. No dramatic encounter with racism or ethnocentrism catapulted me into ministries engaging race and culture. Rather, through most of my life I have experienced the calling of God to address issues of power and relationship that occur in the meeting of people from diverse cultures and races.

Perhaps that consciousness-raising process began in my childhood around our family dinner table while listening to my father's stories. Often they dealt with the struggles of Japanese farmers to reclaim the land they had lost during their paradoxical confinement in internment camps and engagement in military service during World War II. Certainly it was nurtured by the juxtaposition of his stories of Coyote and Salmon and other major figures in the mythologies of the native peoples of the Pacific Northwest with those of the Bible. It undoubtedly intensified during my seminary years while working with the youth of all races and many national cultures at New York's Riverside Church.

These experiences did not really begin to shape my approaches to ministry, however, until the 1970s. Encounters with different learning styles among the students I taught first challenged me to begin exploring the influence of culture on what and how we learn. That quest continues as I seek to understand the persistence of our cultural heritages in the power dynamics of our pluralistic society. In this regard much of my current learning is prompted by the students I teach at Candler School of Theology, in Atlanta, and the racially and culturally diverse group of children I meet each week in the Sunday school of the congregation in which my wife and I participate.

Most of my learning occurs rather awkwardly. Something happens that causes me to see, as if for the first time, some deeply embedded taken-for-granted cultural assumption. Recently, for example, a new consciousness of the contrast in the ways my coteacher from Liberia and I establish boundaries for children's behavior in Sunday school confronted me once again with the influence of U.S. individualism on my teaching. For many years I have taught others that it takes not only a family, but a church and a whole community to raise up a Christian disciple with a public consciousness. Yet when a child transgresses some boundary in our class, I usually account for the psychological and family issues in the child's life before deciding how to respond to her words or actions. By contrast my co-worker pays little attention to the "causes" of the child's behavior. Instead, she calls the parents and draws them into helping the child act in more appropriate ways. How deeply embedded I am—as is my co-worker—in our own cultural perspectives and patterns!

During the 1992-93 academic year, I studied three congregations in Atlanta. This work proved a turning point in my understanding of the power dynamics in the encounters of race and culture. What attracted Ted Brelsford and me to these congregations was their intentional embrace of racial and cultural difference in congregational life. The membership of one congregation, Cedar Grove United Methodist Church, was made up of almost equal numbers of European Americans—many of whom had been long-time residents in the congregation's formerly rural neighborhood—and African Americans, who had more recently moved into the new subdivisions around the church. Oakhurst Presbyterian Church, located in a struggling older suburban neighborhood, had a membership of approximately equal numbers of African Americans and European Americans along with a few people from other racial and ethnic heritages—all with a wide range of economic, educational, and social backgrounds. The third congregation, Northwoods United Methodist Church, also formerly had an almost exclusively European-American constituency. At the time of our study, people from some thirteen nations called it their local church home. The vision, vitality, and witness of these three congregations convinced me (and my research colleagues) that in these congregations we were seeing a direct challenge to the ways most congregations gather and order their lives. Racial and cultural differences were not stumbling blocks to their experience of community; they had become gifts and resources in forming community. In *We Are the Church Together,* we explored the impact of embracing these differences on their understanding of "being church."

Although *Embracing Diversity* also builds directly on the stories of their experience, here I direct attention to the dynamics of leadership. It had been my intention to expand my study of culturally and racially diverse congregations to other communities of faith in preparation for the writing of this book. Other responsibilities prevented me from taking on that task. Consequently the stories of these congregations help order the discussion of leadership that follows. This decision, however, means that the stories I tell will reflect the patterns of racial and cultural dynamics of the southeastern United States in which the historic engagement of black and white racial cultural patterns influences the experience of newer cultural groups from Asia, Central and South America, the Caribbean, Africa, and Eastern Europe. I have visited culturally and racially diverse congregations in metropolitan New York, Chicago, and California and have talked to pastors and read about congregations in other parts of the country. Their stories lead me to believe that these reflections on the experience of diversity in congregational life have relevance to most racially and culturally diverse congregations, but the particular cultural "mix" in any given story may make it feel somewhat different.[2]

I do not take the position that the multicultural congregation should become the model for congregational life in the future. Indeed our study of culturally and racially diverse congregations only underscored the impossibility of such an assumption. The notion of a single model for multicultural congregations, in fact, contradicts the very notion of diversity that they embrace. Regional (geographic) differences in the history of racial and cultural relationship further limit any possibility to find or develop a single model for the multicultural congregation. Even congregations that share polities and doctrines will look, act, and feel different, simply because the way they do things grows out of the negotiations of the particular cultural and racial groups that make up their memberships. We noted, for example, how the interplay of leadership style and congregational life gave a distinctively pastoral character to the ministry of Cedar Grove Church, a prophetic character to the ministry of Oakhurst, and a priestly character to the ministry of Northwoods. And yet the juxtaposition of the historic relationship of southern rural white and urban black Christians at Cedar Grove, their historic roots in the congregational polity of the Methodist Protestant Church, the still rural ambiance of their exurban neighborhood, and the dynamic leadership of a female pastor significantly distinguished this congregation from Oakhurst, Northwoods, and all the other culturally diverse congregations we had the opportunity to visit.

At the same time I came away from that study convinced that these congregations do provide a glimpse of what Jesus might have meant when he talked about the kingdom of God. This past Sunday the Northwoods Church, for example, gathered after the worship service for a fellowship meal to bid farewell to the organist-choir director. A quick glance across the room immediately brought to mind Jesus' parable of the messianic banquet. People seemed to be gathered not only from all the streets and byways of the city, but from all corners of the earth—folks from Fiji, India, Jamaica, Barbados, the Bahamas, Liberia, Sierra Leone, Zaire, and Korea, and other folks whose ancestries would be traced back to Europe and Africa a long time ago. Some children were dressed in school clothes, others in their Sunday best. The clothing of some identified their cultural roots in Africa or India. For those well versed in such matters, one could identify the various Liberian tribes represented by the headdresses of the women. Young and old filled their plates with foods associated with different cultures. Laughing and singing, telling stories. Might this not be an image of a messianic banquet?

A year of study in culturally diverse congregations, however, demolished any fantasy I may have had that these celebrative moments are typical of their life together. Daily encounters with the differences that exist among the people of these congregations provide a persistent confrontation with the depths of the racism in the church and society and the ethnocentrism that exists in almost all of us. Their daily struggles reveal more clearly the dynamics at work in the interaction of the Jews and Samaritans than those related to the visions of heavenly banquets.

It is not easy to give up generations of practice of referring to people with stereotypical names or descriptions. It is difficult to change patterns of deference and expectations of privilege deeply embedded in our cultural bones. So when the pastor of Oakhurst analyzes the racism at work in the schools, the government, the community social services, or the church, as he frequently does,[3] he does so with the recognition that the white folks in the congregation have benefited—even if unwillingly and unwittingly—from that which harms the black folks sitting next to them. Or when members of the Northwoods congregation respond with compassion to the pain of members whose temporary protective status visas have been revoked, many also struggle with new consciousness over the conflict between their support of conservative immigration policies and the suffering of their friends. In the mutual encounter with difference, in other words, our taken-for-granted cultural and racial chauvinism becomes visible to us. We are confronted with the necessity of making a response.

Congregations that intentionally embrace racial and cultural difference may provide clues to how leaders might be more responsive to the diversity that exists in what may look like very homogeneous congregations. Rare is the congregation made up only of women or only of men. Most congregations struggle with the relationship between the young and the older. In most congregations taken-for-granted assumptions originating in differences in educational experience, socioeconomic status, or theological perspective often lead to tension over basic values and concerns. And the typical strategy for dealing with these differences is to provide even more homogeneous settings. So congregations divide people into groups according to age, marital status, sex, and often professional and educational experience. When this happens bankers and lawyers typically end up on trustee committees; teachers end up in the Sunday school, and social workers on some social action committee. The administrative council of the congregation thereby becomes the place where differences in values, perspectives, and tasks are negotiated. In congregations that embrace cultural and racial diversity, that negotiation tends to occur in the broader life and work of the congregation. And in that process a different kind of leadership emerges.

So what does the leadership—both professional and voluntary—of the culturally diverse congregation look like? When asked by The Alban Institute editors, I made the assumption that the answer to this question would be relatively easy to articulate. All I would need to do, I thought, would be to model this book on leadership on any one of several existing volumes on leadership in the church and expand that discussion to account for the diversity of expectations people from different cultures have for leadership.[4] After reviewing our field notes from our studies of Cedar Grove, Northwoods, and Oakhurst Churches and my visits to other congregations across the United States, in Canada, England, Singapore, and Australia and reflecting on recent writings on cultural diversity, I realized that the insights of general books on leadership and congregational management worked in culturally diverse congregations, too. But something else influenced the approaches of their leaders as they sought to motivate, recruit, train, and supervise people for ministries of worship, learning, and mission in the congregation and larger community.

Gradually I realized that the distinctive leadership issues in culturally and racially diverse congregations had little to do with the formal organization of the congregation. They occurred at what I increasingly recognized as the *infrastructure* of congregations. By this term I am focusing my attention on *practices* essential to the creation and maintenance of any group or community. In her definition of *practices,* Dorothy Bass has observed that they consist of "those shared activities that address fundamental human needs"—such as knowing how to talk to each other, negotiating relationships in institutional structures, developing the ties that bind the relationship of people into sustained communal patterns, and ordering a common life—which when "woven together, form a way of life."[5] Typically these practices are taken for granted because we learn them by participating in the community that engages them.

Practices, in other words, give bodily expression to—enact—deeply rooted patterns of meaning shared by the people of that community. These patterns or "webs," as anthropologist Clifford Geertz called them, form the *cultures* that function as "blueprints for the organization of the social and psychological processes" embodied in the symbols through which we communicate with each other.[6] Typically we refer to culture in monolithic terms, as in U.S. or English culture, black culture, or Asian culture. The patterns of meaning through which we symbolize our existence are actually more complex and multifaceted. So, as I introduced myself earlier, I participate in the distinctive yet interdependent patterns of meaning associated with white, Anglo-Saxon, Protestant, North American (U.S.), and male cultures. In reality my world is still more complex. I also see and respond to the world around me through cultural patterns identified with a geographic region of the country, a denomination, a socioeconomic class, and a family. All of us have experience with a diversity of cultures and their practices, but, at this point in history, the encounter of cultures identified with ethnicity and race poses unusually difficult obstacles for leaders of communities. Around these two differences in human experience, our cultural practices have maintained protective boundaries and reinforced ethnic and racial ideologies. This means that when a group of any kind, including a congregation, embraces ethnic, cultural, and racial differences as important components of its self-understanding, the gaps in these cultural practices become powerful stumbling blocks to that task.

Overview

The chapters that follow reflect this insight. The challenge of leadership in culturally and racially diverse congregations requires attention to these practices of communal infrastructure. They are the practices that lie beneath the surface of the liturgical, educational, missional, and administrative functions of the congregation.

The format of the book therefore is relatively straightforward. Each chapter identifies an issue integral to the task of community creation and nurture for congregational leaders. In the first chapter I explore practices that effect the embracing of difference and the implications for the view of church embodied in that embrace. The second chapter examines the practices by which congregations negotiate the differences they encounter among the cultural and racial groups in their constituencies and as subjects of their mission. In the third chapter I explore congregational practices that bind diverse peoples into the experience of community. The fourth chapter is closely related to the third. It focuses on the development of practices of congregational conversation that inform and are shaped by the liturgical, educational, and administrative life of the congregation. The fifth chapter examines the significance of congregational events for ordering congregational life and mission. And the last chapter focuses our discussion on the leadership of multicultural congregations. These last two chapters offer an alternative way of looking at the management of a congregation.

Because culturally and racially diverse congregations are not the product of a theological commission or a denominational mission strategy, pastors and lay leaders do not approach the challenges of creating multicultural communities of faith as experts. Nearly all pastors with whom I talked emphasized that most of what they learned about leading congregations that embrace difference occurred through trial and error. Some have received financial support from denominational offices or governmental grants for special, sponsored ministries. But those same denominations have not developed visions, resources, or leadership training programs to equip congregational leaders to engage in the practices integral to the worship, education, mission, or administration responsive to the cultural diversity they seek to embrace. This book seeks to help fill that gap.

CHAPTER 1

Embracing Differences

At this point in the history of the church in North America, why are a growing number of congregations challenging the historic preference for cultural and racial homogeneity in congregational life?

To answer this question I turn to what I call practices of *embrace*. Ted Brelsford and I began to use this term toward the end of our study of three multicultural congregations. *Embrace* was the only English word we could find that caught up the interplay of differentiation and intimacy in human communities.

After the publication of *We Are the Church Together,* we ran across an essay in which Miroslav Volf used the term "theology of embrace" to describe a framework for mediating the conflicts among ethnic and religious groups in the Balkans. He observed that the act of embracing always involves two movements on the part of two people or groups—a movement to create "space in myself for the other" and an enclosing movement to communicate that I do not want to be without the other in her or his otherness. To embrace others suggests that we cannot "live authentically without welcoming others—the other gender, other persons, or other cultures"—into the very structure of our being. Volf suggested that we are called to embrace others because we are created to reflect the fellowship that exists in the triune God.[1] So when I speak of "practices of embrace," I refer to the movement of different peoples in community that seek to be close to others without losing the integrity of their own identities.

In this chapter I have three purposes: (1) to note that changes in the racial and cultural composition of the United States and Canada create the conditions for the embrace of difference in congregations; (2) to identify four catalysts to the practices of embracing racial and cultural differences in congregations; and (3) to explore practices in these congregations for facing their members' resistance to the presence of racial and cultural diversity.

"Are There Any Other Congregations Like This One?"

Most congregations assume the presence of differing human experience. Their membership encompasses a range of ages and abilities, diverse interests and educational experiences, different marital and social status. Their members may have a variety of religious experiences and hold a range of perspectives on the beliefs they claim to hold. They may be from different regions of the country. The organizational structure of many congregations reveals how much attention church leaders through the years have given to some of these differences. Congregations typically provide educational opportunities for different age and interest groups and rely on a variety of teaching approaches. Sometimes educational opportunities reflect differences in marital status, religious experience, liturgical preference, or theological perspective. A range of congregational organizations provides ways for children, youth, women, men, and sometimes different vocational or professional groups to meet in their own enclaves. Congregations, in other words, affirm the value of certain forms of difference in their common life.

Some differences, however, have proven to be more difficult to incorporate into North American congregational life. These differences—usually associated with race, social class, ethnic heritage, language, and sexual orientation—are perceived to cohere like oil and water; people exhibiting them are perceived to relate to each other about as sensitively as wolves and lambs. Perhaps this explains why the writer of deutero-Isaiah chose these two animals to depict the radical possibilities for his vision of the kingdom of God.[2] This notion of incompatibility, deeply rooted in our collective subconscience and reinforced by structures of oppression, domination, and resistance, usually means that we are surprised if we happen to discover a congregation that does, in fact, embrace any of these differences as gifts and resources to its life and ministry rather than as problems to be avoided or overcome.

Our experience may be like that of a National Public Radio reporter who recently called me. He described a congregation he had discovered in a small Texas city. It had been formed some time ago through the merger of previously "all-white and all-black churches." This merged congregation began its new life with two worship services—one in the style familiar to the members of the congregation with a predominantly African heritage and the other reflecting liturgical patterns deeply rooted in European church life. The congregation has now developed a common liturgy from its separate traditions. The reporter described their anticipation for the first of these worship services. He then asked the question I invariably hear from people who have just discovered such a congregation: "Are there any other congregations like this one?"

In small and large cities across North America an increasing number of congregations embrace differences that in other congregations typically exist as stumbling blocks to a sense of community. This book focuses on the issues of leadership to be found in congregations that specifically embrace racial ethnic/cultural differences as resources to and distinctive features of their common life and experience. The dynamics of leadership in these congregations, I would contend, are not dissimilar to those found in congregations that embrace differences in gender, social class, sexual orientation, or even age as integral to their sense of identity as communities of faith. It often *feels* different however. That difference is important.

In recent years the embrace of *difference*—including differences having to do with racial and ethnic/cultural heritage—in a local congregation's life has something of the quality of a grassroots movement. No visionary leads this movement. No denominational strategy gives it direction. Few congregations have been organized with the intention of embracing racial and cultural diversity. Rather, congregations discover new possibilities for their futures through their responsiveness to people who do not share their racial and/or cultural heritage.

I told the National Public Radio reporter that other congregations like the one he had discovered do exist. I described two for him. One in Memphis involves the recent merger of black and white congregations. The other grew out of the 1970s decision of the leaders of black and white congregations in a small Virginia community to respond to denominational efforts to abolish all vestiges of segregation in the denomination's program and structure. This reporter's feature aired on public radio, and I note that increasingly more stories of racially and culturally diverse congregations are being told in the religious and secular press.[3] These stories often illumine (and sometimes challenge) the theoretical discussions on multiculturalism and political correctness in the media and among scholars. They also provide the catalyst for new discussions on the nature of the church and its ministry among theologians and practitioners of ministry.[4]

Perhaps the editors of the Presbyterian Church (U.S.A.) mission resource book have asked the question that lies behind the growing public attention to culturally and racially diverse congregations and to the dynamics of cross-cultural relationships and communication in them. The text includes a picture of the membership of the Oakhurst Church with the following caption: "What will the Presbyterian Church (U.S.A.) look like in the next century?"[5] A quick glance at the picture reveals the reason for the question. Almost equal numbers of black and white folk of all ages are standing on the front steps of a church building. A visit to the congregation over a period of several weeks makes the question even more provocative. One discovers that the congregation has been working at the task of embracing racial and ethnic/cultural diversity for more than twenty years. Its membership has also included people with Asian, Native American, and Hispanic ancestries. Some members are gay and lesbian. Some depend on welfare. Some give leadership to academic and political institutions in the community. Some have little or no schooling and others have completed their doctorates. The mission statement of Oakhurst reflects the theological commitment that informs its efforts to embrace the diversity in the human community.

> The diversity which we feared has empowered us to confront God's truth in the world. In Jesus Christ the dividing walls of hostility have been broken down. Though we are born into diverse earthly families, our life together at Oakhurst has led us to affirm that we are called to be one family through the life, death and resurrection of Jesus Christ.[6]

Oakhurst, in other words, explicitly challenges the racial, cultural, and economic homogeneity to be found in most Presbyterian congregations. Its embrace of difference is more than a cultural or racial issue. It grows out of an explicitly theological commitment on the part of its members to "proclaim the Good News of the gospel" that "breaks down the barriers of the world" and inhibits the possibility for shalom in human experience.

Will congregations in the United States and Canada in the future *look* like Oakhurst? The demographic changes taking place in many countries of the globe, and especially in the United States and Canada, would indicate that this is not an idle question. The birthrate of people with European ancestry in the United States, for example, slowed to 6 percent between 1980 and 1992 while that of other racial and cultural groups increased by 40 percent. Children of European descent are (or soon will be) in the minority in California, New York, and other large urban and border states. Spanish-speaking Catholics will soon make up the largest language group in that church. The Germanic and Scandinavian heritages of the Lutheran Church and the English heritage of the Episcopal Church are being reshaped by the infusion of new cultural perspectives.

The response of churches to the presence of cultural and racial diversity is not really a new issue. Throughout most of U.S. and Canadian history, congregations have struggled to find faithful ways to respond to the cultural, linguistic, and racial differences of people moving into their communities. Catholic parishes from the beginning of the European settlement have had a "complex, polyglot, and multicultural character." They included "explorers, exiles, captives, and immigrants" as well as Irish, English, French, Dutch, Portuguese, and Spaniards—sometimes all in the same congregation—while being excluded at the same time from the powerful socializing forces in the nation by dominant Protestant perspectives and groups.[7]

Colonial Protestant churches also discovered early in their histories that they could not easily sustain their national ethnic characters. The relationship of European churches to the Native Americans their members encountered and to the Africans many of their members enslaved prompted decades of theological debate over the meaning of salvation, baptism, and church membership. Successive waves of immigrants altering the character of neighborhoods repeatedly presented congregations with the options of opening their doors to the newcomers in their communities, creating new congregations for them, following old members to the new communities where they now lived, struggling to survive with the members who remained, or closing their doors and dying.

Despite the frequency with which congregations—Protestant and Catholic—during the past 150 years have faced the challenge of responding to the cultural and racial diversity surrounding them, a preference for cultural and racial homogeneity continues to dominate their images and expectations for congregational life. Racial and ethnic/cultural homogeneity continues to inform strategies of church growth. The theological education of pastors in most seminaries continues to prepare them for leadership in racially and culturally homogeneous congregations. Denominational curriculum resources and strategies for clergy placement, while more sensitive to racial and cultural differences than they were twenty-five years ago, still perpetuate patterns of cultural homogeneity.

And yet here and there attitudes in some congregations toward cultural and racial difference began to change with the civil rights movement in the 1960s. Growing numbers of people critiqued the adequacy of the "melting pot" image for the national life of the United States because it perpetuated the dominance of a Northern European or Anglo culture both in the nation and in church life. As Lawrence Cremin, a prominent educational and cultural historian, observed, no one with a different racial heritage could live easily into that image.[8] Martin Luther King's vision of black and white children sitting in school and playing together increasingly captured the imaginations of people seeking an alternative way for people of many colors to relate to one another. King's vision reflected more accurately the increasingly popular Canadian image of a cultural mosaic for the relationship of diverse peoples.

Encounters with racial and cultural difference in the 1990s are more complex than the racial dynamics of white and black folk in the 1960s. Demographic realities proliferate the variations in King's vision. The United Methodist congregation I attend includes not only white and black members; its membership includes people from many parts of the globe. In the nearby Catholic parish, people may choose to worship in English, Spanish, or Vietnamese. An English-speaking Presbyterian congregation around the corner now includes cooperating but distinct congregations serving Spanish-, Korean-, and Hindi-speaking peoples. Not far away is an English-speaking Baptist church with ministries in Arabic, Spanish, and Korean. And this is not in California, New York, or Chicago, but in the suburbs of Atlanta. Having noted that, I also see that the majority of the congregations in this neighborhood continue to serve only one cultural, racial, and/or language group. This fact leads to the second question the National Public Radio reporter asked me when he called: "Why do some congregations become racially and culturally diverse?"

For Further Reflection

An Exercise to Name the Diversity in Our Congregation and Community

Directions:

1. To begin to discover something about the racial and cultural composition of the community surrounding your own congregation, ask the local schools for a breakdown of the number of cultural, language, and racial groups represented in the enrollment in each school. One often can obtain a summary of neighborhood census data from the local county or city planning office. Be careful about how you interpret the information you receive. Census and school statistics, for example, often mix cultural and geographic (Hispanic, Asian American) with racial (black, white) categories. One congregation discovered, for example, that the majority of children identified as "white" in the neighborhood elementary school actually came from Spanish-speaking families.

2. To help discover something about the range of cultural differences in your own congregation, take the opportunity when people introduce themselves at meetings, social activities, and educational events to identify where they were born; the places they call home; and the places their ancestors came from. One congregation posted a world map in a hallway and marked the birthplaces of members with colored thumbtacks to visualize the sources to the group's diversity.

Catalysts to Practices That Embrace

Every racially and culturally diverse congregation has its own unusual story to tell about how it began to embrace these differences. When church members complained about the lack of children in the Sunday school of one congregation, for example, the pastor made a special effort to invite the children of neighborhood families to the Sunday school. When these same European-American church members expressed appreciation for the presence of these new children in the Sunday school but bemoaned the lack of "white" children among them, their pastor replied that no one had told her they needed to be of a certain color. Twelve years later the membership of this congregation involved an almost even number of people with African and European ancestries.

In another congregation, the pastor radically altered the future of the European-American congregation he served after hearing the plight of a Hmong congregation that had just been evicted from the church where it had been renting space for worship and education. He invited them to hold worship services in the building of the church he served. He soon asked the board of his congregation why they did not invite the Hmong congregation to become members of the church. The members of the board agreed, and in one Sunday the largest ethnic group in this congregation became its newest. For another congregation, when Spanish-speaking and Vietnamese Roman Catholics moved into the parish, its leaders decided to budget funding for staff members with those language skills to establish ministries for them.

These stories reflect something of the variety in the ways congregations *begin* to embrace differences of race and culture. When stories like these are examined more closely, one can discern patterns among them. In my study of culturally and racially diverse congregations, I have discovered at least four catalysts to the embracing of cultural, racial, and/or linguistic difference in congregational life.

Catalyst 1: Quest for Survival

Some congregations—typically Protestant—begin to embrace difference *in the quest for survival*. They do it out of necessity. A fairly common pattern may be found among congregations that no longer have the economic resources to maintain their buildings or sustain their programs. They embrace difference by renting space to another congregation for the additional financial resources this arrangement provides. The languages and cultural heritages of the two congregations are often different. I think of a European-American congregation that rents space to a congregation of Ghanaian immigrants, of a predominantly African-American congregation that rents space to a Spanish-speaking congregation, of a Japanese-American congregation and an African-American congregation that have made space in their church buildings available to Korean-speaking congregations. Sometimes the host and renting congregations start cooperating in the religious education of their children—especially if the congregation renting space desires an educational experience in English. These congregations may occasionally unite for a special bilingual worship service or share leadership of a mission or evangelism program. Sometimes discussions over the maintenance of church property and its financial support become the impetus to even closer collaboration. The relationship between the two congregations begins, however, primarily as a contractual one.

Catalyst 2: Gospel Commitment

Another catalyst for embracing racial and cultural differences in congregations involves a church's commitment *to preach and teach the gospel to all who would hear and respond to it*. With the growing pluralism of North American society, these congregations have discovered that they no longer have to send missionaries overseas; they can reach out to the cultural "strangers" who now live in their own communities. In this effort culture becomes a strategic resource to communicating the gospel. So the missional congregation will train people to minister locally to newly settled cultural groups in and through their own language and cultural customs. The intent, at least at first, is not so much to bring the resources of that new culture into the worship, fellowship, and educational practices of the missionary congregation, but to share its own cultural encounter with the gospel.[9]

I illustrate this missionary impulse to embrace difference with the example of a European-American congregation that became concerned about the future of the African-American youth in its neighborhood. Building on their perception that a basketball ministry might be one way to keep these youth off the streets, church leaders invested their time and money in that effort. The ministry featured rigorous training in the rudiments of basketball, required Bible study during Sunday school, attendance in worship, and tutoring for school work. African-American leadership was recruited to work with the European-American men who took on this ministry, and together these men encouraged and supported these younger men through high school and many into college. The goals of the ministry were twofold: to help these youth discover and commit their lives to Jesus Christ and to become educated and useful citizens. Elements of their African-American heritage that supported these goals were affirmed. Elements that did not seem relevant to these goals were in some cases ignored (as in preferences in music) or suppressed (as in patterns of speech).

For a congregation like this, the embrace of difference may or may not lead to any increased awareness in its own cultural assumptions and practices. Some congregations may "look diverse." But as one of my students commented after visiting a similar congregation, they can still "feel white." A similar dynamic occurs in black congregations that do not recognize the distinctive cultural gifts of their Caribbean and African members or in Spanish-speaking congregations that do not draw on the resources of the various national cultures present in their memberships. And yet for some congregations, the commitment to share the gospel with others can also lead to the discovery of new cultural resources for their ministries.

Catalyst 3: Hospitality

Some congregations begin to embrace difference as a response of *hospitality* to the racial, cultural, and/or linguistic diversity they encounter in their communities. They strive to make the strangers who visit them welcome; to make room for the differences these new people bring to their common life. Many Catholic and Episcopal parishes, for example, as a matter of course expand their programs and resources to accommodate the language and cultural needs of newcomers who assume the parish church is as much theirs as it is that of those who have been long-time members. A major shift in the Oakhurst Church began when an African American who had been a life-long Presbyterian moved into the neighborhood and decided to transfer her membership to the closest congregation of that denomination. In similar fashion, a Chicago congregation's life and mission was changed forever when a man originally from the Philippines walked by the church building and declared to himself that this would be the church home for his family and friends. Both these people entered into congregational life like guests "expecting to be welcomed." And in both congregations church members searched for ways to make that expectation a reality. Hospitable congregations typically do not expect to be changed by those they welcome into their lives. And yet, as the biblical witness repeatedly indicates, strangers do impact the experience of those they meet. Often they come, as John Koenig has written, as "God's special envoys to bless or challenge us." Their presence, like that of the three strangers visiting Abraham or like that of many people encountering Jesus, reveals some new possibility for the future and often leads to transformation.[10]

Catalyst 4: Theological Vision

A fourth catalyst to the embracing of cultural diversity grows out of the *theological vision* of congregational leaders for a new kind of congregation—one that embodies eschatological expectations for a new kind of community—illumined by images deeply rooted in our biblical and theological traditions. Sometimes these theological visions are intentional and strategic. The Church of All Nations in San Francisco (and later in other cities of the United States, Great Britain, and Australia) expressly embodied Howard Thurman's vision of people from many nations worshipping together. The Riverside Church in New York City, reflecting the vision of Harry Emerson Fosdick, stated from the outset its intention to be "international, inter-racial, inter-religious." Edgehill United Methodist Church in Nashville was organized in the 1960s at the height of the civil rights movement to explicitly live out the dream of Martin Luther King, Jr., as a "beloved community" in which black and white children, youth, and adults might study, play, and worship together.

For other congregations the theological vision emerges from an encounter with difference. A group of white laypeople in a small southern city ran into strong resistance when they sought to implement King's vision of the beloved community in their parish; they left to join a predominantly African-American parish that took them in. A new pastor's first sermon in a congregation in a neighborhood with a rapidly growing number of immigrants from Mexico, Central and South America, Southeast Asia, and Africa offered an alternative image for its future based on the vision of Saint John recorded in Revelation 7—with all the nations and tribes of the world gathered at the feet of the Lamb of God. Challenging the congregation with the possibility of embodying that vision in its own community, he caught the imagination of its leaders. Several months later they voted to become a "multicultural church" without knowing at all what that decision might require of them. That decision started to alter their expectations of what "church" should look, feel, and act like and led them to seek out and welcome the "newcomers" to their neighborhood.

The theological vision of many culturally and racially diverse congregations has been developed into mission statements and summarized in their publicity. Clues to such a vision may be seen in the Northwoods Church's description of itself as "The Church Where the World Worships," or in that of a Chicago-area congregation that calls itself "A Welcoming Community" and then goes further to say that its "membership is open to all without regard to race, nationality, sexual orientation or religious background." The danger for such congregations, of course, is that their vision might become ideological and thereby the source of a new form of exclusiveness.

Summary

The practice of embracing difference *begins* in the everyday responses of congregations to the fragility of their communities of faith: the gospel charge to make disciples of all people, the decision (whether explicit or implicit) to be hospitable to strangers, and the vision of a new kind of community associated with the presence of Jesus Christ. The embrace of difference, however, involves more. It requires the explicit commitment to becoming a new kind of faith community—one that celebrates the gifts of diversity in the ways the group worships God and serves its neighbors.

For Further Reflection

An Exercise to Name Practices of Embrace

Directions:

1. In personal or group reflection, try to name at least one of the following activities in your congregation. Then ponder the implications of your answers for the relationship of people of different cultures in your congregation.

   A. A decision or action to reach a new constituency in the community to help the church avoid a problem or pending crisis—e.g., renting space to meet the budget; starting a day-care program with the intent of recruiting young families.

B. Actions designed to share the gospel of Jesus Christ with people who would not ordinarily come to your congregation.

C. Actions designed to make newcomers with different racial and cultural backgrounds feel at home in your congregation.

D. Official statements on newsletter and bulletin headings; recurring themes in sermons; publicity statements that articulate a theological vision for a racially and culturally diverse congregation.

Facing Resistance

Why do so few congregations embrace racial and cultural differences? And why do so many people—even in those congregations that do embrace differences—find the practice so difficult? To answer these questions we must first remember that racial and cultural difference continues to be a source of conflict and controversy in the United States and Canada. National cultural tensions continue to be lived out in the relation of French-speaking Quebec and the other English-speaking provinces of Canada; Spanish- and English-speaking communities in many cities and communities of the United States; Korean shopkeepers in African-American neighborhoods; and Vietnamese and Texan fishermen. The values and perspectives of regional cultures clash in nationwide church meetings, in the national legislature, in elections, in the culture shock of people who move from one community to another. Debates over affirmative action and the distribution of resources in education and government illumine these conflicts in the media and legislatures of many states. The list of specific examples could continue for several pages. The conflict of cultures has been the subject of many books. This should not be surprising given the histories of the United States and Canada as the destinations for a massive migration lasting more than four hundred years and drawing people from every continent and region of the globe.[11]

Cultural conflicts may be traced to the character of culture. Eric Law reminds us that "each culture has its own characteristics, values, and customs. Some are perceived as strong and some as weak. Some are more aggressive and some are considered passive and timid. People in one culture survive as individuals while people in another culture find their own liveliness as part of larger groupings."[12]

The distinctiveness of our own cultural heritage and identity is deeply rooted in our corporate bones. That which smells good to "my people" may smell bad to the people of another culture. I think of the overly loud comments of a European American about his distaste for the smell of curry in an Indian dish brought to a church supper and of the many times I have heard people from Africa, India, and Mexico talk about how they have toned down the spices to accommodate their cooking to the tastes of their North American friends. A covered-dish dinner in a congregation may, in other words, intensify cultural tensions over the smells and tastes of food.

This experience permeates other aspects of our meeting across cultures. What the people of one culture deem beautiful may not even be noticed by those of another. The musical sounds and rhythms pleasing in one culture may be discordant or irreverent in another. Decisions in a culturally diverse congregation over the decoration of the setting for worship may not be a matter of personal taste but of cultural disposition. People of every culture have distinctive patterns of communication that influence the way they understand the relationships of children and adults and leaders and followers, how decisions are made, and the ways in which the mysteries of God are acknowledged and practiced.

Cultural differences do not occur on the surface of human experience. They are rooted in centuries of reinforced perceptions, practices, sensibilities, and habits in one's relationships to the earth, to others, and to the mysteries beyond human comprehension. They are indicators of the deep thickness of the cultural patterns anthropologists seek to discern in our distinctive identities. Given the depth of these differences, Law compares the challenges facing people who embrace cultural difference to the learning that would be required of the wolf and the lamb in Isaiah's depiction of the peaceable kingdom. It requires becoming conscious of that which is unconscious, of doing that which seems unnatural.[13]

The task is not easy. "Culture hides much more than it reveals," anthropologist Edward T. Hall reminded us decades ago, "and strangely enough what it hides, it hides most effectively from its own participants."[14] Encounters with something different or unfamiliar bring to consciousness that taken-for-granted embeddedness of our own cultural perspectives, values, and practices. The embrace of cultural difference in congregational life is not the same thing as the fascination church people have had through the years with the stories of missionaries from "foreign lands" or with the vacation experience in an "exotic" country. It involves negotiating ways to live with differences that may be not only irreconcilable, but mutually abhorrent and repugnant.

When differences cannot be changed or overcome (as in gender, race, culture, and class), the resistance to negotiating ways to live in solidarity tends to increase. When those differences are reinforced by the systemic forces of racism, ethnocentricism, sexism, and classism, the repugnance of "the other" is intensified both for those who have power and for those who are powerless. For the powerful, the embrace of difference requires suspending the privilege, status, and power they have enjoyed. For the powerless, it involves transforming their patterns of protection and defensiveness into patterns of mutual engagement. The task is not easy for either party. Fear and apprehension are common responses. As Cornel West has observed, in the contestation of cultures in North America, race does "matter" (and so does class, sex, and ethnicity). "Historic inequalities" and "racial stereotypes" are embedded in the structures in and through which people of different cultural heritages meet and interact with one another. As David Hollinger has pointed out, our concentration on body shape and color highlights only certain cultural differences and ignores others; it means that we usually miss the "cultural differences" between a "family of fifth generation Boston Unitarians and a family of fifth-generation Texas Baptists" if all we see is that "they are black. Or white."[15] We cannot begin a conversation on embracing difference in congregational life, in other words, unless we begin with the basic humanness of each of us—that our destinies are bound up more by our shared experience of citizenship in a specific nation and by the common experience of our baptism into the body of Christ than by the divisions of culture and race.

We are familiar with the results of racism and ethnocentrism. Some peoples have been oppressed due to the color of their skin or their cultural heritage. Others have been marginalized to the point that their histories are invisible to the majority of us and often to themselves. Others have been alienated from the roots of their own cultural heritages. These patterns of cross-cultural encounter permeate church structures and processes. We see the consequences of their influence in church policy and practice. Congregations and denominations, for example, have been more willing to send out evangelists and missionaries to convert people who did not share their racial or cultural heritage than to work in the social and political institutions of the nation to ensure justice, freedom, and equity for brothers and sisters of those same people. Theological schools have only recently begun to ask questions about what prospective pastors, Christian educators, church musicians, and other professionals need to know to minister to people who do not share their own cultural heritage. They have only begun to explore the cultural bias in their theologies, in their images of the church, or in the leadership strategies they nurture in their students. Denominational strategies for new congregational development continue to perpetuate cultural homogeneity in congregational life. Even though most denominations now seek to implement affirmative action policies in the selection of their own staff members and elected leaders, few have yet to envision a strategy for developing and maintaining multicultural or multiracial congregations. Indeed denominations do little to implement their policies of racial and cultural "inclusivity" at the local level.

Sources of Resistance

Embracing difference calls church leaders to *face* the racism and ethnocentrism that limit congregational inclusivity. The practice of facing racism and ethnocentrism requires at least two activities: (1) *discerning* ways in which racism and ethnocentrism are embedded in the structures and processes of congregational life and (2) *naming* their presence so as to make it possible for people to make decisions about their influence on congregational life and mission. Congregational leaders may look for racist and ethnocentric resistance to embracing differences in the following sources:

1. Denominational programs and strategies. While often advocating integration or inclusiveness, denominational programs and strategies still perpetuate structures that privilege dominant racial and cultural groups in the church. Because racism and ethnocentricism are embedded in the taken-for-granted structures of our institutions, they are rarely fully uprooted from denominational programs and policies. For example, denominational leaders concentrate their attention on starting congregations in new suburbs—often filled in part by people fleeing neighborhoods going through racial and socioeconomic transition. They give in comparison little attention to denominational support for the role congregations might have in strengthening older neighborhoods or to the mission of congregations in communities experiencing demographic change.

Denominational policies and programs promote models of "successful" congregations drawn primarily from the organizational structures, traditions, and experience of their dominant cultural groups. Criteria for "effective" leadership are based on patterns associated with the dominant culture in a congregation or denomination. Ministry approaches to liturgy, education, administration, and congregational care are drawn from the experience of those with the most power in the congregation or denomination. Curriculum resources, even with authors, pictures, and stories representing different racial ethnic groups, continue to be written in a style and with a format and content that appeals for the most part to the dominant ethnic and racial group that purchases the largest share of the publications.

2. The education and reward systems for lay and clergy leaders in the church. These systems generally do not prepare leaders to value and celebrate difference in their ministries.

Invariably when I address themes of this book in audiences of church leaders, the implicit racism and ethnocentrism of some listeners comes to the surface. Even as some pastors and laity are challenged by the possibilities of being a part of a racially and culturally diverse community, others declare that they would not want to be caught in such a congregation—usually because the task appears too difficult and the threats to their preference for predictability and stability are too clear. I regularly hear complaints from church judicatory administrators about the problems they have replacing pastors who have effectively led their congregations in embracing racial and cultural diversity. Judicatories, of course, have not led any major effort to equip pastors for such placements. I regularly hear the frustration of lay leaders in culturally and racially diverse congregations who sense the lack of attention in church-sponsored training events to the kind of leadership issues they face. I have heard laypeople talk about the rejection they feel when a new pastor from a different cultural group reshapes congregational life around his or her own cultural traditions of faith. Few workshops for lay leaders and teachers begin to explore the sensibilities and practices involved in the embrace of difference in and through their responsibilities.

These concerns are not new to me. In the seminary where I teach, many students deliberately avoid the courses that would best equip them for ministries in culturally and racially diverse congregations and communities. The task of confronting our participation in structures of racism and ethnocentricism often seems too painful to tackle. It requires reassessing the ways we view ourselves and our ministry. It challenges us to learn new leadership skills and sensibilities. And it confronts us with our own complicity in the racism and ethnocentrism permeating our church structures. Our resistance ultimately is located in our desire to avoid the pain of change. But this of course means that we also miss the joy that so many multicultural congregations discover in their diversity.

3. *The preference for win-lose strategies*. This is a third potential source of resistance to congregational embrace of racial and cultural differences. In the making of decisions we are used to seeing a winner and a loser.

Almost every racially and culturally diverse congregation I have visited has discovered that majority-minority voting strategies only perpetuate the experience of cultural margination of any numerically minority cultural or racial group. Most of these congregations have also discovered that consensus strategies also prove unsatisfactory, because they work best when all parties "give up" something for the sake of the whole community. In communities with significant diversity, that which is given up may well be something very important. In a variety of ways these congregations are turning to decision-making strategies that require the participation and contribution of all people and groups. Decisions are built instead of made. This process will be discussed in more detail in chapter 5.

Their discovery is an important one. The very structures for making decisions in a parliamentary democratic approach work best in a relatively homogeneous group or setting. When racism and ethnocentrism permeate those structures, those same democratic processes can all too easily become the means for further oppression.

4. *Fear of losing cultural identity and heritage.* Some people fear they might lose their cultural identity and heritage in a diverse community of faith. This concern is expressed in two ways.

The majority culture may fear loss of their own ethnic cultural heritage. White students in my classes often lament this loss. The melting pot strategies of assimilation all too often discouraged the telling of family stories and the treasuring of family heirlooms through which memories of their past might have been sustained through the generations. Typically they do identify with a national or regional culture, but not their ethnic cultural heritage. The clarity of racial and cultural identity in the people they meet often heightens this sense of loss.

People who have long experienced minority status may fear losing the clarity of their racial and cultural identity that has sustained and supported them through generations of oppression. In a society that historically sought to prevent the transmission of minority racial and cultural identities, congregations have often been the primary agents to that identity's maintenance and renewal. Given the ambiguous motivations for embracing racial and cultural differences in many congregations, it should not be surprising that people in historically marginated congregations might resist efforts to join dominant culture congregations.

For Further Reflection

An Exercise to Identify Racism and Ethnocentrism

Directions:

1. If you are doing this exercise alone, make an appointment to talk with someone in your congregation with a different racial or cultural heritage from your own. If your congregation consists of people from only one racial or cultural group, this person may be from a different part of the country, a different social class, a different type of occupation. Ask this person any or all of the following questions:

    A. In what ways does the ministry of this congregation nurture your faith?

    B. In what ways does the ministry of this congregation not feed your faith?

    C. Where and with whom in the congregation do you feel most free to speak about that which most interests or concerns you?

D. Where and with whom in the congregation do you not feel free to speak about that which most interests or concerns you?

E. Which of your gifts and graces does this congregation most affirm? What gifts and graces does it suppress, ignore, or not know about?

2. If you would like to work in a group, invite several people (probably no more than six or seven) who represent diverse backgrounds and experiences in the congregation to work with these same questions. Be sure to allow enough time for all to share the stories that describe their experiences.

CHAPTER 2

Negotiating Differences

In this chapter I establish the framework for our exploration of the dynamics of leadership in multicultural congregations. In the first section I define my use of the term *congregation.* In the second I explore how the embrace of racial and cultural diversity influences the ways congregations understand themselves to be "church." In the third section I describe four practices for negotiating differences in the ministries of congregations that embrace diversity. I will argue that the term *multicultural* should be applied only to those congregations seeking to embody some form of equity in the power relations of the various cultural groups in the congregation. That equity is essential to the continuity of the identity of the various racial and cultural groups in the congregation and to their collaboration in shared ministries.

Congregations: What Are They?

Congregations, C. Ellis Nelson reminds us, are gatherings of "people who share beliefs and seek to understand and do God's will in the circumstances of their lives." James Hopewell observes that these gatherings of people not only have special names, but over time their members "communicate with each other sufficiently to develop intrinsic patterns of conduct, outlook, and story." Their constant reference to God distinguishes these gatherings of people from most of the other groups or organizations to which they might belong. Gradually they develop corporate personalities or cultures out of the interplay of "their history, location, size, beliefs, and leadership," their sense of mission and "moral obligation" as faith communities, and the dynamics of power at work in the interaction of their constituencies.[1]

Congregations are "local" embodiments or expressions of the church.[2] They locate the actions of church—notably those central to the ecclesial practices of sacramental celebration, teaching, and preaching—in a given place and at specific times. Congregations embody—give form and shape to—historic beliefs, communal practices, and shared perspectives or ways of viewing life and the world. The form and shape of a congregation emerges from the interplay of the cultural heritages and theological traditions of the people in the congregation and its geographic, social, and economic setting. Congregations consequently reveal and express explicitly cultural patterns. Theologies of the church, in other words, are not only received and internalized by congregations; they are also shaped by local circumstance, experience, and practice.[3]

When the members of a congregation share a common cultural tradition and heritage, the interplay of theology and culture in the beliefs, practices, and perspectives of their daily interactions remains, for the most part, relatively invisible to them. They are taken for granted in their speech and actions. Pastors and new members may discern these embedded cultural perspectives and practices in the oft-repeated phrase "We've always done it this way."

When the members of a congregation do not share a common cultural tradition or heritage, they encounter alternative assumptions about the nature and mission of the church as they worship, fellowship, and study together. If these alternative views and practices seem strange, they often become stumbling blocks to the patterns of social interaction required to sustain congregational life. These may lead to conflict over matters of belief, practice, and perspective—especially those related to the ecclesial practices of meeting together, sacramental celebration, preaching, and teaching.

Points of cultural conflict in the ecclesial practices of the congregation rarely begin at the theological level. They originate instead in the realm of personal interactions. A visitor to any given congregation may well wonder how she will be greeted. That question is intensified if its members belong to a different ethnic cultural group or social class. The answer to that question, however, will determine the extent to which she will feel welcome or perceive the congregation to be hospitable. If her expectations of hospitality are met, she may describe that experience with theological terms historically associated with experiential meanings of being church—redemptive fellowship, communion of saints, household of faith, koinonia. Similar questions arise as people encounter alternative tempos and rhythms to the singing of hymns, unfamiliar patterns of prayer, different ways of responding to the sermon during their first visit to a congregation.

When encountering the unfamiliar and unexpected, it's only natural to feel dislocation and disorientation. The meanings associated with particular practices are deeply rooted. I think of some older friends who can appreciate the newer translations of the Bible when they are studying some passage, but when they worship they want to hear the familiar cadences of the King James Version. I have other older friends from several cultural and racial groups who no longer feel at home in church because the images and cadence of liturgies and hymns in new prayer books and hymnals are unfamiliar.

In other words, the presence of cultural diversity in the congregation shifts the attention of congregational leaders from the cultural *transmission* of shared beliefs, practices, and perspectives to *mediating **both*** the *transmission* of particular cultural expressions of faith and the *transformation* of those expressions that arise as people go about the routines of congregational life. This mediating process requires the congregation that seeks to embrace diversity to focus attention on several practices usually taken for granted. They include the following: gathering people into the fellowship of the congregation; embodying the congregation's mission; and linking the congregation's faith in Christ to the cultural experience of people.

Becoming Church

Gathering the Church

Historically congregations have ordered their lives around one of two dominant practices for gathering people into local communities of faith: the territorial parish and the voluntary congregation. Both practices may be traced back to the local experience of church in the apostolic communities of faith that were the object of Paul's attention.

When Vietnamese and Hispanic Roman Catholics moved into a

neighborhood near my home, many *assumed* they would become a part of the local *parish* church. This practice assumes a territorial basis for gathering people into the life of a congregation. Although the territorial parish is unified by the authority of a shared liturgical and institutional structure, as a community with established boundaries it may also accommodate considerable diversity of populace class, heritage, circumstance, age, and condition.

Not far away a Presbyterian church exemplifies the second way a local church has traditionally gathered. This church is made up of four distinct congregations. Although linked by a coordinating council, each worships in its own language (English, Spanish, Korean, and Hindi) and carries on most of its own social and educational functions. Although many members, especially in the original and larger English-speaking congregation, live in the neighborhood of the church building, many others drive some distance. Sidney E. Mead defined this perspective on congregational life as "the voluntary association of like-hearted and like-minded individuals . . . united on the basis of common beliefs for the purposes of accomplishing tangible and defined objectives."[4] The distinctive feature of the *voluntary* image of local church has to do with that choice. Members *will* to fellowship with each other while engaged in a common task. In contrast to the parish congregation in which the corporate life of the congregation gathers into itself individual people who live within the same geographical area, the congregation as voluntary society engages people in building or creating a community of faith out of their commitment to one another with little regard to whether they live near the church building. For this task people chose this Presbyterian congregation not only from among Methodist, Catholic, Baptist, and Episcopal options; they also chose it from among several Presbyterian options.

A third image of the church is evident in a United Methodist congregation located within three miles of this Presbyterian church. It includes people from many nations with quite different expectations for worship and fellowship. Some members who live near the church building look nostalgically back to the days when the Protestant neighborhood church version of the territorial parish dominated the life of this congregation. Other members drive up to thirty miles each way for worship and fellowship, passing by many congregations of other denominations and even congregations of the same denomination. Wade Clark Roof and

William McKinney see at work in congregations such as this one a new impetus to gathering people into churches. It involves a shift of emphasis from shared space or voluntary commitment to shared task—*shared experience.*[5]

They trace this shift to three social movements. The first they have called the "recovery of the experiential" in religious life, in which the authority of personal experience takes precedence in the quest for faith. Members of this congregation, for example, talk about their relationship to one another through their sense of shared intimacy in worship—gathered around the communion table, bound together across racial and cultural lines as they recite together "*Our* Father . . . ," holding hands, and sensing the comforting presence of the Holy Spirit through the symbolic warmth of the place. In this congregation members have made a conscious choice not to associate only with people whose "like heartedness" or "like mindedness" is based on cultural or racial similarities. Rather it has been intensified by the commonality of their experience together.[6]

A second movement also has contributed to this shift. It involves the democratization of the sense of self in which "the categories of race, ethnicity, gender, sexual preference, age, region, physical condition, religious background, occupation, and social class" are being "challenged and discredited as legal and de facto barriers to the pursuit of the self." In this congregation members intentionally challenge racial and cultural barriers in their expectations for the experience of community. When allied with a third movement—to view institutions as existing to serve individual people rather than the other way around—we can identify sources of the congregational members' willingness to envision a future for themselves that they do not see in those around them. Indeed the sense of being abandoned by the denomination because they are no longer successful in more traditional ways has only heightened the shift of this congregation's loyalty to its unique experience.[7]

Over the years in the United States and Canada, these three images for ways in which local congregations gather people into their common life can no longer be so easily distinguished. Beginning in the nineteenth century, Roman Catholics established parishes with overlapping boundaries to accommodate language and cultural differences. In more recent years Catholics (like their Protestant cousins) have in growing numbers searched for congregations in which they (as one friend of mine has said) "felt more comfortable." Through the years, many older Protestant congregations, on the other hand, have taken on many of the characteristics of the parish—except that people tend to call them "neighborhood" or "community" churches. Church members and their neighbors perceive the congregation to be the church home for "everyone" in the area surrounding the church building. Increasingly people enter the lives of both parish and voluntary congregations not only because the congregation happens to be in the neighborhood in which they live or that its members share beliefs and practices, but also because they find that their experiential expectations for worship, fellowship, and mission are met.

For Further Reflection

An Exercise to Identify Practices of Congregational Gathering

Directions:

1. The following questions may help you identify how your congregation gathers people with diverse backgrounds and experiences into its fellowship.

    A. What reasons do people give to explain why they join your congregation?

    B. What reasons do people give to explain why they leave your congregation to affiliate with another—especially if it is nearby?

    C. When active members become inactive, what reasons do they give for the change in their participation?

2. As you ponder the answers to these questions, group them under the following headings:

Commitment to a Common . . .

Place	Task	Experience

3. After reviewing the responses you have listed under each column, which practice for gathering people into the life of your congregation predominates? Is there a difference in the responses of people from different racial or cultural groups?

Embodying Mission

Congregational assumptions about the practices of mission are also challenged by the presence of racial and cultural diversity. C. Peter Wagner, in a thoughtful study of church growth in pluralistic societies, has made this point. He observed that people usually prefer to be part of homogeneous communities of faith, and yet their image of the church's mission often compels them to spread the gospel among people with quite different cultural histories and experience and languages. Consequently many congregations have attempted to embody the mandate to "spread the gospel" not only through mission agencies in other parts of the world, but also to the "tribes and nations" moving into their own communities. This *witnessing* practice of the church's mission emphasizes tasks of starting, nurturing, and building up new congregations and, with increasing frequency, reorganizing congregational life to accommodate two or more cultural or language groups in the same congregation.

The example of the Presbyterian church above is similar to that of the First Church of the Nazarene in Los Angeles. Calling itself a "multi-congregational" church, it witnesses to the unity of the body of Christ in one church by proclaiming the gospel through the languages of each of its several congregations. This approach to the church's mission privileges a view of human nature that focuses on the will as the impetus to community—both in the sense that communities are formed through the voluntary "will to belong" and that salvation involves the submission of our will to that of God's intent.[8] For those congregations guided by this image of the mission of the church, racial and cultural diversity are not obstacles. And yet the missional congregation's lack of awareness of its own cultural embeddedness may be a hindrance to its neighbors who do not share its cultural perspective on Christian beliefs, perspectives, and practices.[9]

A second approach to the church's mission is *service* oriented. It begins with the challenge in Matthew 25 to live out the gospel of Jesus

Christ in our care for the hungry, sick, poor, thirsty, and imprisoned. Congregations that take this mission seriously often find themselves engaged in *service* ministries. The missional outreach of Northwoods provides a good example. Each Sunday morning prayers of thanksgiving and support are offered for those in the congregation who tutor immigrant children in the local school, who serve Meals-on-Wheels to the elderly, who provide a range of services to the staff of the nearby children's home sponsored by the denomination, who volunteer at the only residence for homeless people in the city that tries to keep whole families intact, who make bandages for the Red Cross, who help supervise a soccer program for older children in the neighborhood, and for many more who fill some of the gaps in the social service networks of the city. The members of Northwoods are deeply involved in ministries of care and service. Children and youth join in. The youth fellowship involves the whole congregation each fall in making sandwiches for one of the larger programs for feeding the homeless in the city. All ages—consistently the largest delegation from any congregation in the city—participate in a "walk around the mountain" to raise money for a denominational community ministries outreach program. Although the members freely talk about their church and invite people to come, their motivation for these ministries is not to expand the church membership. It is to serve those who have need of some form of care. It is to be, as more than one person has put it, "the hands and feet of Christ."

Such a commitment to service, similar to the commitment to witness, does not necessarily mean that congregational members will be aware of their own cultural embeddedness in their responsiveness to the human needs they see. When this lack of awareness persists, it can reinforce a paternalistic attitude toward those they serve.

A third approach to the church's mission may be seen in those congregations that seek to *transform* the life of the community. For example, in the 1960s a congregation in Nashville was organized explicitly to create a model of the "beloved community" embracing black and white members of the city. Throughout its history this congregation has at various times challenged civic leaders over issues of housing, jobs, and education and engaged in ministries that sought to reform attitudes and policies contributing to racism and classism. It has sponsored study groups on community issues, mobilized community groups to analyze problems related to housing, schooling, and employment and to develop strategies for challenging governmental leaders and agencies to address those problems. Lay and clergy leaders have been public critics and advocates—modern-day prophets over issues of injustice and oppression.

Though one particular image of mission may predominate in a congregation, all three may be present. Many congregations motivated by the necessity of witnessing to those who have not heard the good news of God's saving grace are deeply involved in local social service ministries. Congregations serving a range of human needs may find themselves in ministries of public witness in the quest to alter the spiritual ethos of the community, or they may undertake strategic action to alter certain racial, political, and economic conditions affecting the people they serve. And congregations, like the one in Nashville, are also deeply concerned about the quality and character of the relationship of individual people to God. But these practices of mission do influence congregational attitudes toward the diversity in human experience. Each may lead to highly empathic ministries by individual members. Each can also perpetuate paternalistic approaches to ministry. But several generalizations can be made: Congregations emphasizing a mission of witness tend to share Wagner's conviction that cultural homogeneity rather than cultural diversity will better serve their missional strategies.[10] Congregations seeking to transform the social structures that perpetuate racism, classism, sexism, and the other "isms" of oppression and domination are more likely to see the need for the kind of transformation in themselves that will embody their missional goals in the larger community. And while service-oriented congregations may nurture in the people they serve a personal relationship to Jesus Christ and work to improve their social, economic, and political situation, they also tend to emphasize direct acts of compassion and care.

For Further Reflection

An Exercise to Clarify Practices of Embodying Mission

Directions:

Individually or as a group, identify the places where various members of the congregation are engaged in some missional effort. Which practice of mission most influences their different efforts? List each activity that you identify in one of the columns below. Do the people in different racial or cultural groups approach missional activities in similar or different ways? After listing your answers to these questions, assess which practice is most influential in shaping the mission outreach of your congregation.

Mission Practices of . . .

Witness	Service	Transformation

Linking Christ and Culture

A third set of practices at work in being church is brought to consciousness in congregations that respond creatively to the diversity in their midst. These practices originate in the shared congregational convictions about what H. Richard Niebuhr called the relationship of Christ and culture.[11] Niebuhr was intrigued with how our understandings of Jesus shaped our view of culture. He directed his attention to this relationship in the writings of theologians rather than in the practices of congregational life. Niebuhr viewed the dynamics of culture through the insights of mid-twentieth-century theorists. He thought about culture in rather static terms emphasizing artifacts more than processes; products more than the dynamics of cultural interaction. He did not ponder, for example, what happens when Christians encounter multiple cultural options through which they might meet the Christ, nor was he attentive to the ways in which culture influences our perceptions of the incarnation of God in Christ. Consequently his writing reflected the posture of dominant cultural groups who tend to view religious meanings and practices through the lens of their own cultural experience. Their cultural perspective functions normatively in their judgments about other cultural religious traditions and experience. The tension this creates in the culturally diverse congregation occurs, therefore, not only at the point of cultural patterns of social interaction, but also in cultural perceptions of the meanings of significant theological ideas.

In contrast I share the fascination of contemporary missiologists with how our cultural experience influences our perception of Christ and how theology is shaped by its cultural context. Theologian Robert Schreiter, for example, has described three cultural perspectives that I have found useful in understanding the cultural embodiment of theological ideas in the practices of culturally diverse congregations.[12]

The first practice seeks (1) to "free the Christian message as much as possible" from the cultural accretions members bring to their encounter with one another's faith traditions and experience and then (2) to "*translate*" or make sense of that message in their own situation. I see this pattern at work in the Northwoods Church. During the past year the congregation has sponsored several events designed to provide opportunities for people from one racial/cultural group to describe to another the cultural, social, political, and religious context that shaped their faith journeys. So on one Sunday Liberian members introduced us to indigenous foods, discussed the contemporary crises in Liberia by exploring some of the political, economic, and religious forces at work in it, sang hymns frequently heard in Liberian churches, and shared some of their own faith stories. Another Sunday our attention centered on the experience of Christians in India. In another program we explored cultural differences in the faith journeys through Lent of members from Liberia, South Carolina, Jamaica, and Mexico. This prompted further sharing by people from Panama, Wyoming, and Barbados. In this process members of this congregation are discovering not only how each cultural group prefers to pray, sing, and talk about how God works in its life, but each group also tries to translate its experience of the gospel into terms the rest of the congregation can understand.

A second practice seeks to *adapt* historic ways of expressing the Christian message to the thought patterns, images, and practices of local cultures and groups. As with the first practice, churches have been engaged in adapting the Christian message for centuries. G. Ronald Murphy describes a fascinating example in his study of the epic poem *Heliand.* Written in the ninth century by an unknown author, it sought to reimage the gospel in terms familiar to newly converted Saxon Christians. The text brings the Saxons into the story of Peter who becomes a "knight-companion" to Christ and thereby an acceptable model for the Saxon warrior noble. In this effort the author seeks to retain "orthodox Christian teaching," and yet he also transforms the Gospel through the use of Saxon religious imagery and values.[13]

The process continues in churches today.[14] A simple illustration occurred in several congregations as members confronted the pervasiveness of traditional "white" images of Jesus and other biblical figures in stained glass windows, in pictures hanging on the walls, and in Sunday school curriculum. Oakhurst Presbyterian Church has taken an adaptive stance in relation to these visual images. After a prolonged and often heated discussion, the session of the congregation voted to darken the image of Jesus and some of the disciples in the stained glass window over the choir loft in front and to leave the "white" image of Jesus in the window over the back balcony. The basic Western European aesthetic structure of the original window remains, but the effect of darkening the image of Jesus in the most visible window transformed the function of that image in the racial and cultural politics of that congregation. The darker image is up front and center. The theological messages conveyed by this action are reinforced by the Sunday school teachers who color in the pictures of people in the denominational curriculum to balance the presentation of racial and cultural images the children will see in those resources.

Adapting practices are often evident in the conscious and unconscious decisions about how a congregation will sing a hymn such as "Amazing Grace." Which cultural perspective and approach to the singing of this hymn will prevail? In a congregation with members of African and European descent, will the congregation follow the rhythms and harmonic patterns typically associated with African-American or European-American worship practice? Will the congregation alternate or vary the patterns by which it sings this and other popular hymns? The answer to these questions will reveal something about the way a culturally and racially diverse congregation adapts the various cultural understandings of the ways God acts in and through our lives.

Schreiter uses the word *contextualization* to describe his third theological practice responsive to the role of culture in shaping the Christian message. Contextualizing practices begin with "the needs of a people in a concrete place," and from there move to "the traditions of faith."[15] This pattern is especially evident among congregations that seek to embrace the variety of differences among their members as gifts to the task of being and becoming church. In this practice the embrace of difference tends to heighten pastoral and church leadership consciousness to the cultural biases in its interpretations of scripture, theological traditions, and church governance. At the same time it encourages leaders to honor the range of cultural perceptions and approaches that the various cultural and racial groups bring to the discussion. This practice, in other words, requires what Letty Russell has called a "standpoint" perspective on the interplay of biblical and theological texts and their shared experience of their particular church and community context.[16]

An illustration of this process occurred in a Bible study among the students in a class I was teaching on culturally diverse ministries. We were working with the story of the Syrophoenician woman found in Mark 7:24-30. The line of the story is straightforward. Jesus has entered a foreign country—Tyre—the only time the gospel writers indicate that he did so. He was preaching, teaching, and healing. A woman who was a Gentile—a foreigner—came up to him to request that he heal her daughter. He refused. She responded by quoting a proverb with a highly graphic image: "even the dogs under the table eat the children's crumbs" (v. 28, NRSV). Jesus commended her faith and told her to return home. When she did, she found her daughter had been healed.

Most commentaries on this passage make the point that this passage legitimated the mission of the church among Gentiles for people in the early church. The students, however, looked at the passage out of the contrast of their own cultural and social locations with those of the story's characters. Members of the class included women and men of European, African, Hispanic, and Korean descent. The gospel story recorded the presence of the Jewish Jesus, the Galilean disciples, the Syrophoenician woman, and what may well have been a Gentile crowd. More reflection brought to our attention the gospel writer's own Jewish cultural and social perspective, and the dominance of male Western European scholars in the history of the interpretation of this text.

After examining the story from the standpoint of each of these people in the text, someone newly observed that in this instance, "Jesus was being rebuked by a Gentile woman for the narrowness of his mission." The text from this perspective not only legitimated the mission of the church beyond the Jewish Christian community, but it also emphasized that Jesus could learn something about the mission of the church through a woman and a Gentile. This reading of the text, in other words, "authorized" the voices of women and outsiders to the dominant cultural and religious group in the text—and in the class itself. It thereby upset implicitly assumed notions about the location and exercise of the power in the multiplicity of cultural and gendered voices in the class and in the churches they represented.[17]

The practice of contextualization emphasizes the importance of hearing and honoring the variety of cultural perspectives and approaches to some ministry or task of the church. It also draws on those same perspectives and approaches in the ways in which it develops its own theological statements in liturgies and ministry plans. The experience of the Northwoods Church while developing a congregational mission statement illustrates this process of contextualizing the gospel in the interplay of the cultures of the congregation. The process began much as books on management suggest. The administrative council voted to develop a mission statement. It also agreed to hold a council retreat to start writing the statement. A time was set that would make it possible to ensure a good representation of ages, cultures, and length of membership. The retreat began with Bible study and prayer. A definition of a mission statement was given. The group then brainstormed possible themes and issues to be included in the statement. These were discussed and prioritized. A committee was appointed to develop a first draft. Several weeks later the committee brought its proposed draft to the administrative council. Up to this point there had been little that was unusual about the way the Northwoods Church approached the task.

During the meeting, however, someone asked if the mission statement truly gathered up the views and concerns of the various groups in the congregation. Rather quickly members of the council agreed that they could not be sure about the answer to that question. Someone suggested that the statement be circulated to each Sunday school class beginning with the youth classes, the circles of the women's society, and the other committees of the congregation; that it be discussed during the time usually allotted for announcements prior to the prelude for the Sunday worship service; that it be included in the weekly newsletter sent to the entire membership; and, perhaps most important, that members of the council call the members of the church who were not a part of any of the Sunday school or committee structures to discuss the mission statement with them. This last step acknowledged that people from different cultures view publicity in quite different ways. Members from some cultures take the written authority of letters and newsletters seriously. Members from other cultures rarely read these general announcements. If something is important, they expect to be told in person.

Suggestions made during this process were given to the committee, which revised the draft and brought the new version to the administrative council. The statement was discussed again and sent back through the church for a final reading. Again the committee reviewed the comments, did some editing, and brought this draft to the council, which voted to approve it. The process required the contribution of the total membership—the entire community—not to ensure that all voices had been *represented*, but that they had all been *included* in the final draft.

In summary, congregations that begin to take seriously the racial and cultural diversity of the people they serve often challenge taken-for-granted assumptions about what it means to be church. They are confronted with the need to make again—and sometimes over and over again—decisions about how to gather people into their congregational life and work, about how they understand and practice mission, and about how they will relate to the interplay of cultural perspectives on the gospel and their common life together.

For Further Reflection

An Exercise to Discern Practices Linking Christ and Culture

Directions:
Individually or as a group, explore the following questions:

1. In what ways do the understandings and practices of the cultural group with the most financial and organizational influence shape (a) the content and style of worship, (b) the way you teach and learn together, (c) the way and the times you socialize together, or (d) the manner in which you conduct church business or make decisions for your corporate life?

2. When and where have some groups attempted to translate their experience of the gospel for people in other groups? List in the column of *translating practices* found below.

3. When and where has the congregation adapted certain cultural traditions, beliefs, or practices for its own ministries? List in the column of *adapting practices* found below.

4. When and where has some congregational effort attempted to take on the point of view of another person or group on its own terms with the

expectation that both members or groups will discover or experience something new in the process? List in the *transforming practices* column below.

5. Which of the three sets of practices most characterizes the approach(es) of your congregation in making sense of the relationship of theology and culture? Explore whether or not you would like to work on developing more skill in one of the other practices.

Linking Theology and Culture

Translating Practices	Adapting Practices	Transforming Practices

Dynamics of Power in Negotiating Differences

The introduction of ethnic cultural and racial differences into congregational life radically alters the power dynamics in the interaction of congregational members. Power dynamics similarly change in any congregation that seeks to democratize its approach to gender, sexual orientation, social and economic class, physical ability, region, or theological perspective. The dynamics of power become visible in the simplest interactions of people who do not share a common racial or cultural heritage—often during their first meeting.

How shall people greet each other? Will they firmly grasp hands and then simultaneously move them up and down together, or will they grasp hands in a series of moves that ends with a firm grip of thumbs, or will they grasp hands so as to create a snap with their fingers? Will their greeting include a bow or the touch of cheek to cheek? If so, how deep will each person bow? Which cheek and how many times will they touch each other's cheeks? Will they look in each other's eyes or at the floor? Is a hug or "high five" appropriate? Does age or status influence what they say and do in greeting? Most actions of greeting are conducted unself-consciously in a culturally homogeneous group or community.

We learn to greet each other by being greeted. When we meet someone from a different culture, however, we become almost instantly self-conscious about our habits of greeting. These habits are important. They indicate welcome and acceptance, and their absence conveys rejection and hostility. The patterns of greeting, in other words, can tell the outsider much about the dynamics of power in a culturally diverse congregation. Does one cultural pattern consistently prevail when people from two groups greet each other? The pastor of one congregation instructs the congregation after the benediction to give each other "a handshake, a hug, or a kiss" legitimating in the process several cultural approaches to greeting each other. That invitation, however, still does not address the individual *power struggles* that occur when members of different cultures greet one another. Something as basic to community life as greeting one another lifts into congregational consciousness ways in which power is exercised and experienced.

That consciousness may move beyond patterns of greeting to learning how to make decisions about shared activities and programs that account for varying cultural assumptions about the allocation of resources and the nature of leadership. Eventually church members have to address issues deeply rooted in the histories of their relationship with one another. Consequently congregations of people with African and European ancestry discover, for example, that the deepening relationship among members brings to consciousness ever more complex consequences of the dynamics of slavery and slave holding—of segregation and racism and prejudice—in their decisions about what hymns to sing, what foods to prepare for a covered-dish supper, how and whom to nominate for offices of leadership, and how to make sense of the relationship of the stories of exodus and incarnation in sermons and Bible study groups.

Congregations that negotiate cultural differences originating in the values and practices of slavery and slave owning will face different issues from the members of another congregation that includes soldiers who fought in foreign lands and people whose homelands have been ravaged by war. Different congregational mixes will bring different issues to the fore. For example, what does the veneration of Mary involve in a parish with communicants whose religious memories are grounded in German, Italian, and Mexican pieties? Or what kind of religious education for children will people seek in a congregation that includes people who have always been associated with a Christian culture and others who have lived as a religious minority in a Muslim, Hindu, or Buddhist society?

The new consciousness of cultural diversity emerging from these negotiations radically affects what Fumitaka Matsuoka has called the power dynamics of congregations. Communities that embrace difference (rather than seek to inhibit or limit difference) engage in a radical shift in the power dynamics integral to both autocratic and democratic patterns of organizational life.[18] The prophet Isaiah observed that this shift has an eschatological character (Isaiah 11). It leads to the possibility that wolves and lambs might dwell together, children might play freely over the homes of poisonous snakes, and cattle and lions would eat side by side. The power dynamics of culturally diverse congregations metaphorically chastens the tendency in "wolves" to ignore the fear of "lambs" who have experienced years—perhaps centuries—of their aggressive and dominating ways and requires them to alter their carnivorous ways. It also challenges "lambs" who have traditionally avoided or submitted to "wolves" to assume new ways of relating to structures of power, to take on new roles and responsibilities. Meat-eating lions radically alter their behavior to eat grass with cattle. And cattle overcome their fear to mingle with lions.

Any movement toward this "peaceable kingdom" comes in small steps. Those steps will probably not begin until that point in time when people who have been traditionally marginated or oppressed can trust historically dominant groups enough to risk themselves and their cultural heritages. An example occurred one Sunday in the congregation I attend: Several years after joining this congregation, a Liberian member decided to instruct the rest of the congregation on the "proper" way to greet a Liberian. To challenge the dominant patterns of a group can be daunting. To work for changes that might make a group more accepting of difference can be risky. Even more frightening are the challenges to the dominance of certain theological ideas or notions. So when Oakhurst decided to darken the color of the face of Jesus, the issue was hotly debated. The vote to change the image of Jesus was a slim one. Some people left the church. For those who remained, their image of themselves as a church had been transformed.

There's nothing new about the power dynamics evident in the encounter of diverse cultures in congregational life. Congregations have struggled with appropriate ways to respond to diversity in their life together from the beginning of the Christian movement. In the writings of Luke and Paul, we find clues to contemporary possibilities for culturally diverse congregations. Luke portrays a Jesus who consistently challenges conventional wisdom about God's relationship to people on the social and cultural margins. A *Roman* centurion's faith, for example, is as acceptable to Jesus as the faith of any Jew (Luke 7:9). A culturally despised *Samaritan* exemplifies the neighborliness we should seek if we are to live into the second great commandment (Luke 10:25ff). A *Cyrene* foreigner carries the cross of Jesus (Luke 23:26). Perhaps the paradigmatic example for diversity in the congregation occurred at Pentecost when all the Jews gathered in Jerusalem from all over the known world heard in their own languages Galilean disciples proclaim the gospel (Acts 2).

A persistent theme in Paul's letters similarly has to do with altering the power relationships of Jewish and Gentile Christians. He challenged the Corinthians to see in the contribution of their spiritual gifts, wealth, and religious/cultural heritage the interdependence essential to their life together as the *body* of Christ (1 Cor. 12:12-13). He did not distinguish between Jew and Gentile when he called all the members of those struggling new congregations "brothers and sisters." Across their differences, they had more in common "in Christ" than they did with any "unbelievers."

Contemporary congregations continue the struggle with issues of cultural diversity. The issues do not tend to be confined to the relationships of Jews and Gentiles as much as they are evoked by our encounters with people from "all the nations and tribes" of the earth who now live side by side. Contemporary responses to the experience of racial and cultural diversity in congregations seem to fall into at least four practices of negotiating the power dynamics across cultures. These four practices are described below.

Sponsoring Congregations

Within five miles of my home are a Presbyterian, a United Methodist, a Catholic, and three Baptist churches that each *provide a place* for at least one other congregation or ministry distinguished from its own

European-American heritage by language and culture (Arabic, Korean, Spanish, Vietnamese, Chinese, and Hindi). In a sense each church sponsors a new congregation in its facilities and through its ministries.

The view of the relationship of the gospel to culture in these sponsoring congregations, however, reveals the power dynamics among the various groups in the congregation. When churches make room in their building for congregations or ministries for people who do not share the dominant cultural heritage of the congregation's membership, the groups tend to live alongside each other rather than to interact on a regular basis with each other. Their interactions tend to occur in the negotiations over the use of space and times of meeting rather than over the content and practice of worship, education, or mission. The sponsoring congregation usually holds on to as much power over the future of their relationship as possible—as in the authority to terminate rental contracts or to hire and/or dismiss staff members. The nesting congregation, however, may just as strongly protect its autonomy to conduct its ministry in its own way and to terminate the relationship if it does not work out.

Cultural differences are honored in their particularity. In other words, sponsoring and nesting congregations are expected to engage in their own cultural practices. The cultural dominance of the sponsoring congregation is not questioned—especially by its own members. Few people other than the pastors and the officers of the church are involved in the conversations around these negotiations. These conversations tend to expand to other people and over other topics only at points where the groups experience tension or conflict with each other. A frequent source of such tension is the use of the church nursery when residual prejudices and diverse assumptions about child care surface or when the activities of one group conflict with those of another due to differences in the way they understand time. Eventually the leadership of the different groups may build some trust with each other. At that point the sponsoring and nesting congregations may jointly plan a bilingual worship service or develop a pattern of cooperation for the religious education of children. Sometimes the congregations involved develop a shared administrative structure for the oversight of shared concerns and ministries.

Several assumptions about the interplay of culture in congregational life may be found in the relationship of sponsoring and nesting congregations. Cultural differences are assumed to be a part of God's creation.

Those differences are to be honored. But the dynamics of power in the relationship of sponsoring and nesting cultures is hierarchical. That relationship allows racial and cultural privilege to persist in the attitudes of sponsoring congregations and perpetuates the sense of margination and oppression among the nesting congregations even as it honors their cultural integrity. The culture of the sponsoring congregation is privileged in the political and missional dynamics of congregational life. Sponsoring congregations are *multicultural* in as much as they recognize the demographic presence of different cultures and honor the integrity of their cultural differences. But they do not, as a rule, question their own cultural dominance in their negotiations with the congregations nesting in their facilities and ministries.

Transitional Congregations

A United Methodist congregation on the edge of a large metropolitan region illustrates a second pattern of cultural negotiation at work in culturally and racially diverse congregations. A little more than ten years ago a developer laid out a subdivision near this small rural congregation that had served the European-American families living on the farms surrounding it for more than 150 years. Other subdivisions followed. Within four years housing tracts dominated the landscape, and the congregation actively invited the European Americans moving into these new homes to become a part of its fellowship.

The rapidly growing congregation voted to build a large family life center and education building. Even as the new building was nearing completion, the first African-American family moved into one of the nearby subdivisions. More followed. Soon an African-American woman began worshipping with this congregation. Church members welcomed her with considerable ambivalence. Many realized they needed to recruit a significant number of new members each year to help (among other things) defray the expenses of their new building.

But then for-sale signs sprang up in all the subdivisions around the church. The pastor reported to me that at one point half the membership of the church had their homes for sale. Increasingly the typical buyer was African American. The European-American membership of the church declined as members sold their homes and moved away. Unless something happened to counter the demographic changes occurring around this congregation, it became clear that its cultural identity in the future would differ from that of its past. When the European-American pastor's request to be moved was granted, the bishop's appointment of an African-American pastor to the radically diminished congregation also signaled to the community that this congregation was now "free" to become a "black" congregation.

In this scenario we can see a second pattern of cultural negotiation at work in congregational life. Here church members seek to maintain the institutional viability of their congregation as its cultural perspectives and practices shift from one cultural group to another. Given the racial dynamics at work in U.S. communities, the most visible examples of transitional congregations among Protestants involve the transition from a predominantly European-American to an African-American racial and cultural membership. Among Roman Catholics the transition more often involves the shift of membership from predominantly European-American to Hispanic constituencies. But the pattern has little to do with any one race or culture. Rural congregations on the edges of expanding cities face uncertain futures as the newcomers in subdivisions replace older families. An Episcopal congregation that once served its predominantly African-American neighborhood gradually realized it had a future only if it reached out to the Spanish-speaking people moving into it. A historic Japanese-speaking congregation that had invited a Korean-speaking congregation to use its facilities discovered over time that, as its own members continued to move to distant suburbs, the future of the church in that place depended more on the rapid growth and expansion of this new congregation.[19]

Several assumptions inform congregational approaches to the power dynamics of living in communities in transition. First, congregations reflect their cultural contexts; indeed they are the recipients of the blessings of those contexts in good times and the victims of their suffering and pain in bad times. In this regard congregations tend to respond passively to the social, political, and economic changes that surround them. They experience themselves as powerless in the face of larger social and economic forces.

A second assumption is similar to one found in sponsoring congregations. People prefer culturally homogeneous communities of faith. The power dynamics in transitional congregations generally center on the efforts of long-time members (1) to preserve their congregations as viable faith communities in whatever form they may take, (2) to perpetuate as many of their traditions and customs as possible through their new members, and (3) above all to ensure the continued use and upkeep of cherished church buildings.

A third assumption has to do with the cultural negotiations of the outgoing and incoming cultural groups. The former makes enough accommodation to assure the latter that they are welcome, without sharing much power with them, until that point when some action—typically the appointment or selection of a new pastor—signals to all that the congregation is now to be identified with the new cultural group. In other words, the assumption is that cultural difference leads inevitably to conflict. The role of leaders is to do all in their power to ameliorate or reduce the tension as the congregation changes.

Transitional congregations are *multicultural* only in the sense that for a time people from different cultural heritages coexist while they negotiate the transfer of power and of church from one group to another. Although the people in these two groups may develop deep friendships and share significant experiences of ministry together, their relationship tends to function more as a phase in the congregation's life. When the transfer of power occurs, members of the original cultural group tend to experience a deep sense of loss. A layperson, hearing that his European-American pastor would be moved by the bishop and no doubt be replaced by an African-American pastor, revealed this mood when he asked his pastor: "They [the church hierarchy] have given up on us, haven't they?" The feeling of the newer group, however, is the opposite. Excitement and anticipation of a different future—one more familiar to their religious and cultural heritage fills their imaginations.

Assimilating Congregations

When the new pastor of Northwoods United Methodist Church first drove down Buford Highway, in northeast Atlanta, to see where he and his wife would soon live, he was surprised by the number of shops and restaurants with signs in Korean, Chinese, Spanish, and Vietnamese. The territory was new to him, and he decided to preach his first sermon from the text in Revelation that depicts all the nations and tribes of the world gathered around the throne and the Lamb. Many members of this all-white congregation in a community where elementary-school children spoke more than twenty different languages at home almost immediately caught the implications of this vision for the future. Northwoods did reach out into the community and invite its new neighbors to join. Many of the newcomers who responded were immigrants. Some were refugees, fleeing war-ravaged homelands. Some long-time members did not share this new vision and left for other congregations. Those who remained were excited by the possibilities of reinvigorating the congregation. But at first they did not expect that they would be changed by the presence of these newcomers.

Assimilating congregations nearly always move so-called minority or marginated peoples into a dominant-culture congregation—not the other way around. Few European Americans seek to join or *integrate*—the primary strategy for assimilating congregations—an African-American, Korean-American, or Hispanic congregation. Few African Americans join a congregation of Jamaican or Nigerian immigrants, and few European Americans or African Americans join a predominantly Hispanic congregation. And in an earlier day few Irish would seek to integrate an Italian congregation. Dominant-culture folk do not usually choose to affiliate with groups that have less status or power. In assimilating or—in the popular U.S. vernacular—melting pot congregations, the "wolves," or dominant-culture folk, expect the "lambs," or minority-culture folk, to learn to think, act, and relate to each other like "wolves."

In congregations with a significant immigrant membership, as in Northwoods, many long-time members saw their efforts as a way of helping their new members become productive citizens. In other words, the assimilating congregation continues to live out of a mission objective often articulated during the 1920s to assimilate immigrant newcomers into the national identity that happened to include a Christian orientation to life. This process of assimilation has dominated the U.S. imagination for many decades. Both newcomers and oldtimers have often expected those who are new and different to shed that which does not fit their new cultural situation—including the theological perspectives that informed their old faith practices—to become a "member" of this particular Christian fellowship.

An assimilating strategy is most evident in congregations in which the numbers of culturally different "newcomers" are relatively small in number. At this point a subtle but powerful distinction must be made. More and more assimilating congregations welcome people without regard to race, but that does not mean these congregations embrace the gifts of the ethnic and cultural heritages of their new members. In an essay on a similar dynamic in the schools, Signithia Fordham describes this process of personal acceptance and cultural suppression as a strategy of "racelessness." Her point is that to avoid the "stigma attached to being Black, and to achieve vertical mobility," some black people adopt a personae that indicates "a lack of identification with, or strong relationship to, the Black community."[20] A similar process may also occur for any cultural group that happens to be in the minority in an assimilating congregation or group.

When the "newcomers" become a visible presence in the congregation—when they make up what some have called "a critical mass"—they may refuse to continue to act like the dominant group and insist on the inclusion of some of their own values, customs, and practices into the life of the church. At this point the congregation may opt to become a transitional congregation, or it may struggle toward a future as a multicultural congregation in which the contestation of cultures is seen as an important value.

Multicultural Congregations

The story of Oakhurst Church illustrates yet another way of becoming a racially and culturally diverse congregation. For several years Oakhurst could easily have become a transitional congregation. The call of a new pastor, however, led the congregation in a different direction. The congregation included black and white members, and it quickly became apparent to him that the white members continued to hold the power. White members dominated the offices of leadership, and the keys to the locked doors of the church were tightly controlled by a small group of white folk. At that point the new pastor seized authority of the congregational committees to equalize the racial and cultural balance of power among the elected leaders. The shift in the power relationships between European- and African-American members was symbolized by a new distribution of keys, making the church building accessible to all newly elected officials. Those actions altered the character of the negotiations between black and white church members. Increasingly African-American members challenged hegemonic notions and practices of their European-American colleagues—always within the ritual framework of shared joys and concerns during worship, potluck suppers, and committee meetings. After several years the session felt ready to write the mission statement we have already briefly described.

Similar stories are being told by Catholic and Protestant congregations not only in the United States and Canada, but also around the globe. As the number of newcomers increased at Northwoods, for example, long-time members discovered that the newcomers did not really assimilate into the established church-life but rather influenced the way the congregation worshipped, socialized, and conducted its business. At first these changes were subtle. Contrary to congregational custom, some new members did not arrive for up to thirty minutes after the worship services or Sunday school classes had *started*. Many of the newcomers had different assumptions about the place of children in the church, about the authority of older adults, and about the practices of stewardship.

In the multicultural congregation these differences do not remain stumbling blocks as they do in assimilating congregations. Instead, they are engaged and often embraced as resources for the creation of a new kind of community. Some Northwoods folk, for example, arrive early or before the designated time for worship and other activities. Others arrive thirty minutes after the designated starting time. When the worship service lasts seventy-five or more minutes, some people feel like "church" has hardly begun and others feel it has "gone too long." But when the pastor invites folk to give one another a "hug, handshake, or kiss" after the benediction, late arrivers and those who are ready to leave greet one another with warmth and affection.

In *We Are the Church Together*, Ted Brelsford and I described this experience as "the suspension of expectation." The practice has theological overtones. In a multicultural church, the vision of a messianic banquet as portrayed in the Gospels is seen not so much as an eschatological hope but as an eschatological reality. The focus is not on the display of cultural heritages but on their interaction. In this experience we may discern an emerging image for what we are calling the multicultural congregation. In this use of the word "being multicultural" focuses on the interaction of the peoples from diverse cultural groups.

A different consciousness emerging from these negotiations of power embodies a radical theological shift in a congregation's understanding of the meaning of being church. This shift is reflected in a phrase I have heard from laypeople across the country. The old phrase often heard in assimilating congregations emphasizes that beneath race or culture "all people are the same." The new phrase has a variety of wordings. Two of the most common are "God loves us in our differences" and "We are a mosaic of God's creation." Jesse Jackson has described such a community as a "rainbow coalition." Each phrase seeks to emphasize that one cannot experience the whole if any part is diminished or obliterated.

In a study of the dynamics of teaching and learning in the pluralistic classroom, C. A. Bowers and David J. Flinders remind us that ecological metaphors more effectively describe our experience of diversity. They note, for example, that every classroom includes an ecology of diverse language patterns and cultural styles. The culture of the classroom, in other words, grows out of the interaction of multiple patterns of speech, ideas, and actions. The multicultural congregation in similar fashion embodies the interplay of diverse ways of speaking, thinking, acting, and believing deeply embedded in the particular cultural traditions of its members. The ecological metaphor is an important one. It emphasizes the interdependence of cultures in the life and work of the congregation rather than dominance of one culture over the others.[21]

The change of consciousness that underlies this shift in the ecological politics of diverse congregations Ted Brelsford and I tried to capture in the phrase "embrace of difference." The practice of embracing others is not easy—especially given the human proclivity to exclude, dominate, differentiate, and oppress people who are considered to be other and to privilege and give preference to ourselves. It begins with discerning difference as a possibility—a gift—rather than a problem. It continues with the recognition that our lives and our cultures are inextricably intertwined and interdependent—even though when examined discreetly they often seem to be studies in contrast. It requires the affirmation of cultural "others" on their own terms and, at the same time, an affirmation of our own cultural embeddedness as a primary resource to the depths of our own identities. This requires that members of each racial and cultural group grant the others "sufficient respect" to listen and trust enough to challenge and critique. This cannot happen without sharing power, creating a collaborative engagement on the issues that matter most in the common life of the congregation.[22]

For Further Reflection

An Exercise in Negotiating Difference

Directions:
Individually or as a group, list relationships or actions in your congregation that seem to fit the above descriptions of the following practices for negotiating differences. After you have completed your list, compare it with the public statements congregational leaders make about the ways in which racial and cultural groups relate to each other in the congregation. Are they congruent or contradictory? Do your lists reinforce the image you would like to project for the congregation? If not, what issues must be addressed by congregational leaders?

Practices of Negotiating Difference

Sponsoring	Transitional	Assimilating	Multicultural

CHAPTER 3

Congregational Ties

Blest be the tie that binds
Our hearts in Christian love;
The fellowship of kindred minds
Is like to that above.

In the eighteenth century John Fawcett wrote the words to this familiar hymn. It has been a favorite in many congregations. When sung at the conclusion of a service of worship, it reminds the assembled congregation that a bond deeper than any in human experience will sustain their fellowship while scattered throughout the community during the week. When sung at a funeral, it reminds worshippers that their relationship to each other through Jesus Christ cannot be broken by death. When sung in a congregation embracing racial and cultural diversity, the words point to a new kind of community—one that shatters the notion that racial and cultural homogeneity are necessary for the bonds of congregational life. In these congregations the ties that bond people across racial and cultural difference are not just eschatological promises; they are daily experiences. But establishing or creating the ties that gather such diverse peoples into a fellowship of Christian love is not an easy task.

A Linking Practice

A Lutheran pastor of a culturally diverse congregation in Chicago illustrated this point during the coffee hour after a Sunday morning worship service I attended. He told me his ministry was "constantly linking people with each other." It did not take long for me to see what he meant. We had been talking for only a moment or two when he excused himself. He walked over to a young couple he had never met; they were standing off to the side by themselves. He introduced himself. He talked with them long enough to discover they had recently come to Chicago from the Cameroons; they had been students in Lutheran mission schools, and the young man was now enrolled as a graduate student in theology at one of the local seminaries. He then took them across the room to another couple. He introduced them and provided enough information about something they shared in common to get another conversation started. He moved on to a long-time member of the congregation who had recently taken responsibility for a new ministry. After a few minutes of conversation, he suggested that she meet a new and younger member with whom he had been discussing concerns related to this ministry. He made sure they remembered each other's names, explained to the younger person the older person's role in the ministry, and identified enough of the younger person's interest in the project to get their conversation started. After leaving them he stopped for a moment to make sure I felt comfortable, and then he moved on to another person. When I left some forty-five minutes later, he was still moving from one person or group to another, "linking" people, as he described the process. In the words of the hymn, he had begun the process of establishing the ties that bind people in fellowship with one another.

This pastor had developed a strategy for affirming and embracing the racial and cultural differences in the congregation he serves. The difficulty of the task is real. Each group in the congregation has deeply embedded memories cautioning members against associating too closely with the strangers of other families, cultures, nations. In the contemporary climate of "fear of strangers," highlighted by media reports of crime and violence, the task may be even more difficult.

Despite Paul's admonition that in the eyes of God no difference exists between Jew and Gentile, people continue to gather into congregations bound together more by the commonality of family, racial, and ethnic heritage, language, and social class than by shared acts of praising God. Nearly fifty years after the beginning of the civil rights movement, congregations continue to be among the most racially segregated institutions in U.S. society. Indeed cultural and racial homogeneity would seem to be a dominant characteristic of congregations in the United States and Canada.

An important "truth" underlies our human resistance to gathering across our differences. Our identities are rooted in our cultural heritage. Shared linguistic patterns do inform the ways we look on the world around us, discern God's activity in human history, and shape our interactions. Time-honored cultural patterns establish rhythms of relationship binding us to one another in the familiarity of their repetition.

Seeing Strangers as Neighbors

But as Christians our vocation grows out of our responsibility to be neighbors to one another. The gospel writers underscore in several ways that Jesus expanded the prevailing notion among the Jews and still among us about whom we are to view as our neighbors. They are to include those we despise (the Samaritans), those we oppress (the sick, the imprisoned, the poor), and the powerless (widows and children). Indeed we will experience the presence of the Christ most clearly in our neighbors. This would, of course, include those whose racial and cultural heritage differs from our own. Our neighbors, in other words, include anyone who is different from or strange to us.

A stranger is someone who is not known to us; someone we have not seen or heard before; a newcomer; someone who is not usually in this place or does not fit the situation. The word is often compared to "alien" or "foreigner"—identified with another (not this) place or tribe. The most common human responses to "strangers" range from curiosity to fear. We are fascinated by that which is strange to us when the newness is not threatening. We fear those who are strange to us when we are not sure what they will do or demand of us. And that fear, the popular media insists, is not necessarily unwarranted. Daily it conveys messages that strangers are agents of suffering, pain, and death.

Recognizing Strangers as God's Agents

John Koenig points out, however, that a contrasting view runs through the biblical record. From Abraham's encounter with the three strangers to the chance conversation with the unknown traveler on the road to Emmaus, the stranger from a biblical perspective may be an agent of

God's blessing or challenge. In Matthew 25 the gospel writer identifies Christ as the stranger we meet in the hungry, the naked, the imprisoned. Strangers, from this perspective, "enlarge our total well-being rather than diminish it." Koenig continues to point out that the major festivals of the church—Christmas, Easter, and Pentecost—"have to do with the advent of a divine stranger." In each instance a stranger brings blessing that cannot at first be understood, and yet when received, brings hope and transformation to our human experience.[1]

A subtext in the biblical view of the stranger emphasizes God's embrace of all nations of people. God speaks to and acts for humanity through those who were considered foreigners or strangers—a Moabite woman becomes the ancestral mother of Jesus; a Syrophoenician woman expands Jesus' vision of his mission; a Roman centurion becomes an example of faithfulness. A list of these surprising agents of God could be lengthy. The paradigmatic embrace of all nations, however, occurred at Pentecost when Jews from all the known nations of the world heard in their own tongues the Galilean disciples praising God. Some years later Paul the apostle would dramatize the "strangeness" of that new experience of community in his description of the relationship of the Jews and Gentiles in the Corinthian congregation as "members one of another." Contemporary congregations embracing people from diverse cultural and racial heritages continue to live out of that experience of hope for community embodied in that image for the church.

Embracing Strangers

The challenge of embracing the strangers we meet in our own communities and congregations, however, does not occur in the abstract. It emerges from the interactions of people from diverse cultural groups in the daily comings and goings of our life and work together.

This challenge was underscored for me during a conversation with a pastor serving a congregation of people whose ancestries could be traced back through the European immigration and the African diaspora, and people who had recently come to the United States from thirteen different nations in Africa, Europe, the Caribbean, South America, the South Pacific, and Asia. Although the children and grandchildren of many long-time members visit from time to time, the congregation has only five three-generation families—three with European ancestries and two from Liberia. That is to say that the ties contributing to the ethos in this congregation do not rely on the bonds of kinship.

Cultural assumptions about the relationship of children and adults in community had to be identified before the members of this congregation could affirm the differences they experienced among themselves. Tension existed between members whose ancestors had come to the United States and those who had more recently immigrated. More specifically, tension existed between those who assumed parents had primary responsibility for the behavior of their children and those who assumed that the responsibility for the behavior of children belonged to the adult who was closest to them. These differences may appear negotiable on the surface. People on both sides could affirm their differences. But when it came to their feelings about how the others responded to the actions of children in church, they related more frequently as total strangers to one another.

Awareness of this cross-cultural tension only heightened this pastor's sensitivity to the challenge of preaching, teaching, and caring in this congregation. He noted that he could not assume a common, shared cultural, much less religious, background. (Members had been drawn from United Methodist, Baptist, Lutheran, Presbyterian, Catholic, Church of God in Christ, independent Pentecostal, as well as Muslim and Hindu traditions.) Ethnic cultural differences—even for the members of different tribes from the same African nation—intensified the range of options for hearing and responding to any words he said or decisions a committee might make. Perceptual screens rooted in racism, ethnocentrism, classism, and contemporary forms of nativism could easily subvert the best of his intentions for the relationships of the people in the congregation.

He has learned that some people in the congregation will hear his words as he intended them. Other people will hear them out of the particular cultural and religious experiences they bring to their hearing. This same dynamic is at work in the communication patterns among church members. So this pastor cannot assume even the dominance of a given cultural ethos for the patterns of communication integral to the act of worship. Although he was describing a different sociocultural dynamic at work in contemporary life, Robert Worley's image of the church as a "gathering of strangers" aptly describes the experience of congregations that intentionally embrace the diversity of humanity.[2]

And that experience encompasses both the fear of the unknown and the anticipation of the possible permeating the familiar biblical stories about strangers.

The metaphor of the stranger consequently provides a helpful way of describing the processes through which congregations embracing human diversity nurture the ties that bless their experience of community. In our study of culturally diverse congregations, those processes might be clustered under three sets of leadership practices. The first focuses on welcoming strangers—a ministry of hospitality. The second centers around gathering strangers into the fellowship of the congregation through bonding rituals of mutual acceptance. The third explores what it might mean to live out of the gospel possibilities for the congregation as a "company of strangers" celebrating the interplay of solidarity and diversity.

Welcoming Strangers

Signs of Hospitality

Three things immediately caught our attention when we started visiting the Cedar Grove Church in Atlanta. Every Sunday we were greeted at the door by two men—one black and the other white. Each welcomed us, and one or the other would give us a copy of the liturgical bulletin for the day. We later discovered this was not a coincidence. The visible interdependence of the black and white leadership of the congregation was carefully orchestrated by members of the nominating committee—because they wanted to present that image to newcomers and to prevent themselves from falling back into patterns of associating primarily with people "of their own kind."

As we walked into the sanctuary of the church, we could not help but notice the three stained glass windows to our right. When we asked about them, we discovered they had been commissioned by the congregation during a remodeling project a few years before. One window depicts Jesus' encounter with the Samaritan woman at the well. In the middle window Jesus is surrounded by four children—two with dark skin hues and two with light. The third window depicts the two disciples who ignorantly argued over the privilege of sitting at the right hand of

Jesus in the kingdom of God. Again we discovered these themes had been intentionally chosen to communicate to all who visited this congregation that those most welcome were those on the margins, those who experienced oppression, those who sought but had not yet recognized Jesus to be the messiah.

The third thing to catch our attention was the pastor standing up after the prelude and announcing: "Welcome to Cedar Grove Church. We are family here." We had a sense of what that meant following the worship service, as black and white folk stood around talking to each other for more than thirty minutes. The pastor's statement, according to Elliot Eisner, an educational theorist, exemplifies the *explicit* messages that every congregation uses to describe itself.[3] Explicit messages of welcome convey what congregations want people to know about themselves. They are found on the signboard outside the church building, on the masthead of liturgical bulletins or congregational newsletters, and in the names of Sunday school classes. The Northwoods Church for example, describes itself as a "church where the world gathers to worship." I previously mentioned a congregation in Evanston, Illinois, that states in a flier for visitors: "Spiritual seekers, regardless of racial, sexual or religious orientation are welcome." The explicit intentions congregational leaders seek to communicate through phrases such as these are expanded into mission or vision statements and embodied in congregational programs and structures. Chris Argyris has called these statements of intent "espoused theories." They communicate to everyone what we say we believe about ourselves.[4]

Eisner observes that any curriculum for teaching and learning, and we might add any congregation dedicated to worship, mission, and fellowship, also communicates *implicit* messages that may or may not be congruent with their explicit messages. These implicit messages can either reinforce or contradict the explicit messages of welcome. The fellowship of diverse peoples engaged in conversation over an extended period of time conveys implicitly something about the character of the fellowship in that congregation. The notion of the Cedar Grove Church as a racially and culturally diverse family takes on an even more surprising twist when read through the stained glass images of a woman who is an outsider, black and white children, and arguing disciples. The presence of these images poses, at least subconsciously, the question for the newcomer to the congregation: Does this community of faith welcome—indeed embrace—people typically marginated and powerless? These windows do not portray heroes or heroines of faith. Instead they honor people more typically associated with experiences of oppression—a woman from among the despised Samaritans and children—and they lift into our consciousness one of the least grand moments in the journey of the disciples with Jesus to the cross. These visual messages provide a persistent implicit message that this congregation may have an unconventional way of relating to the structures of power in society. Our greeting at the door reinforces this perception. No one announces that this congregation welcomes "black" and "white," but the presence of white and black greeters underscores the explicit message that racial and cultural homogeneity is not the way this congregation defines itself.

Signs of Hostility

When people in congregations wonder why people do not return after a first visit, they are usually unaware that two other dynamics are at work. First, the explicit and implicit messages of welcome may contradict each other. My wife and I experienced this conflict of messages in a congregation we attended after moving into a new community. During the worship service each Sunday morning, one of the pastors extended a welcome to visitors. His words were always warm and his attitude friendly. After the service people around us would greet us, but no one would strike up a conversation with us. When we tried, it usually ended after the exchange of a sentence or two. When we reached the door, a pastor usually asked a question that indicated an awareness of something going on in our lives. He made us feel welcome. Then we would walk to our car, perhaps with a wave from someone we had seen before. At weekly Wednesday evening fellowship dinners, we had a similar experience. A host officially welcomed all who had come. The pastors engaged us in conversation. The people with whom we sat introduced themselves, asked us for our names, and then turned to each other to carry on the conversation they had begun as if we were not present. We are not shy people. We do not have difficulty initiating or sustaining a conversation. But despite its overtly friendly greetings, we experienced this congregation's fellowship as exclusive and distant. I know that if we had had the time to teach a Sunday school class or volunteer with some other church project, we would have been able to talk with others about that common task. But we were both stretched to establish our new home and start new jobs. This congregation intended to be friendly, but we experienced our acceptance as being quite probationary. The implicit message of conditional welcome undermined the pastor's explicit messages of unconditional welcome.

I see a second dynamic that keeps people from returning to a congregation. In workshops I am frequently asked why people with different cultural heritages so often do not return to a church after visiting. The question usually goes something like this: "We go out of our way to be friendly. We take time to talk to those who visit us. We send them the newsletter of the church. Someone from the church visits their home. Why don't they come back?" When I probe the situation a little, this second dynamic often appears: The implicit messages beneath explicit overtures of friendliness are experienced as hostile. This occurs when people never see a face or hear an accent like theirs in any leadership role; when they receive no instructions for following an unfamiliar order of worship; when they do not hear any awareness of their human situation reflected in the stories or the themes of the sermon. In other words, the congregation may greet visitors but not include them. Whether or not a congregation intends to do so, this lack of responsiveness conveys more of a sense of hostility than hospitality to the newcomer. To avoid any confusion in this regard, the pastor at Cedar Grove explicitly told visitors they were "family too."

From Hostility to Hospitality

The movement from messages of hostility to hospitality is required for congregations seeking to embrace the strangers they find in their communities. The difference is seen in comparing the posture of the Prodigal Son's father—standing out on the road expectantly waiting—to the posture of the sulking brother, refusing to participate in the banquet. Hospitality, Henri Nouwen has observed, occurs when we look for the promise of relationship in our guests. This anticipation removes "artificial" distinctions between us as we reach out to the strangers in our midst and invite them to be our friends. Hospitality in this sense involves the "creation of a free and friendly space" where we can discover the possibilities of reciprocal mutuality.[5]

The creation of that space in culturally and racially diverse congregations requires a growing consciousness of the variety of cultural assumptions about the meaning of hospitable space. This tension takes at least two forms. In the Cedar Grove Church the intention was to convey the message that all people are welcome. But some people do not feel comfortable in a setting in which "everyone" is welcome. They prefer to associate with people they know. Even if they like the preaching, the music, and the activities for their children, the preference for homogeneity is more powerful. The welcome of the congregation that embraces racial and cultural diversity may be experienced as judgment rather than as invitation.

These tensions over differing cultural assumptions regarding what is hospitable occur at the most basic levels of our interactions. Earlier I have described the ambiguity facing the members of the Northwoods Church over how they should greet one another. On a recent Sunday the pastor of this congregation explored the implications of this ambiguity for the future of the church. He noted that when visitors who had grown up in African or Caribbean cultures came to the church, they felt more fully welcomed when they had the opportunity to stand up and be introduced to the congregation. In contrast, he observed that young professionals born in the States visiting the congregation for the first (or even the fifth time) did not want to be singled out for attention. Follow-up calls to several white young professionals who did not return after an initial visit invariably turned to the embarrassment they felt when "forced" to stand up and give their names. This discovery has led the congregation's leadership to explore ways to recognize and honor the differences in expectation people have for being welcomed. This process makes explicit the implicit cultural assumptions people bring to their association with one another.

Signs of welcome crossing the traditional boundaries of race and culture must necessarily function at a deep level if they are to counter the ever-present dynamics of racism and ethnocentrism. They must reveal that differences are valued; that the experience of diverse peoples is honored; and that the power dynamics of congregational life have been altered to celebrate the contributions of each racial and cultural group. Creating signs of welcome is perhaps one of the most important tasks taken on by congregations seeking to embrace racial and cultural diversity.

For Further Reflection

Exercises to Reflect on Practices of Welcoming Strangers Who Are Neighbors

The following exercises are designed to be used by committees and groups seeking to understand the extent to which their congregation is a welcoming community of faith. Each includes guidelines for gathering information and for making decisions about what is found.

Exercise 1: Seeing Ourselves as Others See Us

Directions:
Every congregation communicates a number of explicit and implicit messages about itself to people who walk or drive past the church building and visit it for the first time. This exercise involves the collection of those messages by small groups of two or three. A small group works best because we tend to see more when we are in conversation with others. The exercise can be divided so that different small groups focus on different sets of messages.

Step 1: Collecting Information
Look for words, pictures, and architectural features both in and outside the church building that say either "welcome" or "not welcome." Check these specific places:

A. On the street(s) approaching and around the church building.
B. In the entryways.
C. In the hallways and on bulletin boards.
D. In class and meeting rooms.
E. In the place where people gather to worship.
F. In bulletins, newsletters, and published brochures.
G. In curriculum and resources used in educational classes and church ministries.

Step 2: Analyzing Information
If working in a group, post the information collected in step 1, so everyone can see it. Then on a new sheet of paper list the groups of people that are explicitly made to feel welcome; implicitly welcome; explicitly not welcome; and implicitly not welcome. Note especially any messages that might say "welcome" to members and "not welcome" to nonmembers.

Step 3: Making Decisions for the Future
Review your answers in step 2. Then identify which messages need to

be changed and what new messages need to be added. Complete this process by deciding who will make these changes, how they will be done, and by what date.

Exercise 2: Making Room for Strangers Who Are Neighbors

Directions:
We know we have been fully accepted when we are included—as the parable of the messianic banquet makes clear—at the head table. In this exercise you will look for signs of this kind of acceptance of the different racial and cultural groups in your congregation. Here you will gather information of a different kind. Use the following questions to explore the extent to which signs of welcome have become signs of acceptance. After gathering this information, identify strengths and problems in the ways your congregation accepts the presence of racially and culturally diverse people.

1. What racial and cultural groups are represented in the membership of the choirs? To what extent does the membership of the choirs reflect the diversity in the congregation?

2. What racial and cultural groups are in visible leadership roles during the worship service? Identify the leaders and the roles they fill. To what extent do these leaders reflect the diversity in the congregation?

3. What racial and cultural groups are in visible leadership roles in other aspects of congregational life (such as the educational program, fellowship dinners, committees, social action groups)? To what extent do these leaders and the groups they represent reflect the diversity in the congregation?

4. Review the list of officers for the congregation. How many of the cultural and racial groups in the congregation are represented by their presence? What are the four most influential offices in the congregation? Which racial and cultural groups are represented by officers in those positions of leadership?

5. Identify cultural and racial seating patterns during worship, fellowship meals, committee meetings, and other congregational gatherings. To what extent do people move back and forth from their own racial and/or cultural group to mingle with people from other groups?

Gathering Strangers into Community

Oakhurst Church does not begin its worship service with the familiar call-and-response greeting. Instead the pastor invites the congregation to gather itself in a ritual practice of greeting. Following his words of welcome, the assembled congregation stands. Young and old, black, white, brown, and yellow, welfare recipient and college professor, long-time member and, after some initial hesitation, first-time visitor rise to their feet and weave their way through the pews and clusters of people to shake hands, share hugs, and exchange words of greeting and fellowship. On my first visit a nine- or ten-year-old enthusiastically greeted me as if I were a long-missing friend. As I looked around almost everyone was similarly caught up in this burst of friendly interaction. Oakhurst folk do not simply turn around to greet those seated nearby; they move around the room. Most try to touch everyone present at some point. This ritual practice rarely takes fewer than ten minutes. When explaining why it took so long, the pastor told us that most people have not seen each other for at least a week. The congregation draws people from a wide geographical area. He observes that the congregation in this scattered state does not become a "body" until people have had the opportunity physically to touch each other. At that point they are much more likely to be emotionally and spiritually *gathered* into the experience of community central to the act of *corporate* worship. Touch, reinforced by words of greeting, gathers their disparate attention into common focus on the act of worship.

His words point to an important insight for contemporary congregations. Historically, parish congregations included people from a common geographic area. When they gathered to worship, their meeting together had been intensified by their interactions with one another all week. In this situation, regular liturgical events functioned as the heartbeat of the community, pulsing regularly in the midst of the ebb and flow of daily and weekly activities. They gathered in and sent people out into the community where their lives were already intertwined.

Traditional voluntary congregations gathered people whose common commitment to a particular confession of faith, liturgical style, or missional task provided a focus for interactions. Their loyalty to each other grew out of that which they shared. Their gathering renewed and intensified that commitment to each other through that common enterprise or task.

When contemporary congregations gather, more likely than not, their members neither see one another regularly nor enjoy a common commitment to some task or even the same belief system. They come disconnected from one another. Yet they seek some sense of being linked to one another, some bond of fellowship. Many congregations have responded to this quest by borrowing strategies for ministry from the entertainment industry. They focus on technologically reinforced "performance." Those who do the work of worship are staff members who produce and manage ministry options for the congregation. The corporate experience of being "church" in this situation is similar to the shared catharsis of a concert or powerfully made movie. Congregations like Oakhurst, in contrast, understand the body to be a corporeal reality in which touch, talk, laughter, and tears become the bonds that link people in fellowship.

The Practice of Gathering

In its ritual practice of greeting, Oakhurst signals an important shift in the organizational life of churches and other social groups in North America. In parish and voluntary congregations, leaders assumed a constituency for congregational events and programs. Leaders would plan an activity for the life of the congregation—often with great care. They would then *announce and publicize* that event and wait for people already loyal to the place and/or mission of the congregation to come. And historically, among those who identified with those congregations, a significant number of people would come. If people did not show up, two causes were typically identified: either the event did not speak to the needs or interests of people or the publicity was inadequate. Publicity effectively gathers people to a common place in parish and voluntary expressions of church. It relies on a prior sense of belonging to the same community or fellowship.

I suggest, however, that publicity is no longer an adequate strategy for assembling a congregation for liturgical or any other activity. Because prior relationships rarely are compellingly deep, they are not enough either. People participate only if they are *gathered* into the momentum of the experience they anticipate. The commitment to the ministry possibilities in the event and to others in the community must be nurtured. The dynamic of gathering strangers may be seen in some so-called megachurches in the "movement psychology" that informs strategic decisions about anything the churches do. People participate because they sense they have become part of something bigger and greater than they are.

The phenomenon is also seen in the greeting practice of Oakhurst. This congregation does not assume that its fellowship is strong or pervasive enough to bind its members into persisting community. Indeed the practices reflect the assumption that culturally diverse congregations are fragile fellowships that constantly and attentively need to be renewed and intensified. That binding process must occur on a regular basis. The experience of community that builds from the initial act of mutually greeting one another continues through the liturgy and is finally named at its end when members of the congregation leave their seats to create a gigantic circle around the sanctuary while singing "There's a sweet sweet spirit in this place." A sweet spirit does bind young and old, black, brown and white, male and female, gay and straight, affluent and poor, highly educated and illiterate, while members hold hands and sing together.

A similar ritual process provides a rhythmic pattern of acceptance at Northwoods. The liturgy in this congregation builds to the climactic moment after the sermon, after the offertory, to the invitation to gather around the circular communion rail at the center of the sanctuary for what church members call "altar prayers." This liturgical moment involves a bidding prayer of intercession for people in the congregation, the community, the nation, and world. People asked by the pastor articulate these prayers on behalf of the congregation; then the pastor asks those gathered to take their neighbors' hands as they begin praying together "*Our* Father...." Hands of all colors, all ages, male and female, from many nations randomly assembled around the communion table clasp while they pray together. At the conclusion of any other meeting or gathering, members of the congregation similarly create a circle, hold hands, and pray. And so their touch renews and intensifies the bonds of fellowship they experience in their weekly gatherings for the worship of God. These are rituals of acceptance.

Rituals of Acceptance

A ritual of acceptance may be defined as recurring experiential actions that communicate to those involved that they are unconditionally incorporated into the fellowship of this gathering. They belong to these people. They are connected to this place.

Rituals of acceptance are most fully embodied in the sacramental life of the congregation—especially in the sacraments of Baptism and Eucharist. In racially and culturally diverse congregations, the sacraments' messages of God's unconditional acceptance may deepen or intensify the acceptance people experience from one another across the boundaries of race and culture. And yet the binding potential in the sacraments of Baptism and Eucharist in the culturally and racially diverse congregation cannot be taken for granted. The celebration of each can also evoke social and cultural patterns of rejection. The baptism (or dedication) of a child, for example, does not simply convey the incorporation of that child into the fellowship of that congregation. It involves the public acceptance of that congregation's responsibility—as an agent of God's unconditional love and grace—to raise up that child. In a congregation of diversity in which no one set of assumptions about how a child is to be raised can be found, that ritual act tests the depth of that congregation's quest to participate in the body of Christ.

A congregation in Ohio recognizing this challenge altered its practices surrounding the baptism of children. It instituted an educational process for each family and indirectly with the total congregation. When parents requested that a child be baptized, a member of the clergy visited the home. This visit centered on helping the parents or guardians to recall their own baptism and to reflect on the meanings they associated with the experience of baptism. On a second visit the clergyperson interpreted that congregation's theological understanding of baptism, its biblical sources and liturgical expression. On a third visit the clergyperson brought a member of the congregation who would serve as its representative in the baptism itself. When this person's racial or cultural heritage happened to differ from that of the family, the event directly challenged any residual racism or ethnocentrism affecting relationships in that congregation. During this third session the parents or guardians would describe their dreams and hopes for the child, their fears for the future of the child, and their hopes for the congregation's involvement in the raising of the child. Invariably their hopes had to do with the difficult tasks parents face in raising children in a pluralistic, materialistic, and impersonal society. During the baptismal liturgy these hopes and fears were shared with the congregation. They were reported to the appropriate committees of the congregation, especially when existing patterns of church life could not provide support to the family involved. The sheer repetition of this process over the years significantly heightened the centrality of this ritual process in the worship life of this congregation and enhanced the concern of adults for the well-being of their children.

For Further Reflection

An Exercise to Identify Significant Rituals of Acceptance

Directions:
Ask up to ten people of different ages and from different racial and cultural groups in your congregation to describe which ritual actions heighten their sense of belonging to the congregation, intensify their sense of being fully accepted by others, and deepen their sense of connectedness to the love and grace of God. What do their responses tell you about the effectiveness of your practices of acceptance?

A Company of Strangers

The Quest for Solidarity

When the worship committee of Northwoods Church decided to draw on its increasing racial and cultural diversity to celebrate Pentecost, it did not have a clue about the consequences of such an event. The Northwoods story provides some helpful insights to our discussion of the processes of nurturing the ties that bind very diverse peoples into community. The planning process began several months prior to Pentecost Sunday. It included several critical components.

1. Cochairs were appointed to lead the process. They represented two of the more than thirteen racial and cultural groups in the congregation.

The membership of the committee reflected even more of the congregation's diversity: male and female; from youth to older adult; several cultures; and a range of formal educational and religious experience.

2. Committee members took plenty of time to get acquainted. They shared stories of their faith journeys and described the worship practices that had meaning for them—including those they did not experience in this congregation.

3. The members took time to study carefully New Testament and other theological texts explicating the experience and meaning of Pentecost—with special attention to the sermon Peter gave on that occasion.

4. The committee then planned a liturgy for Pentecost Sunday drawing on the variety of liturgical and devotional traditions familiar to the congregation's members.

5. Committee members took responsibility for explaining the significance of Pentecost and describing their plans for Pentecost Sunday in the church newsletter, during the general announcements in the worship service, and to the Sunday school classes.

6. Members of the committee recruited readers and leaders for the various parts of the liturgy. They asked Sunday school classes to rehearse the hymns they had chosen, urged people to read the original story of Pentecost in their Bibles, and requested that everyone arrive early for worship during the Sundays prior to Pentecost Sunday so they could rehearse elements in the service. All who had leadership roles, from acolytes and readers to ushers and choir members, were urged to come to the church on Pentecost morning prior to the Sunday school hour to rehearse the liturgy. As many as half of the typical attendance for worship were involved in some way.

7. The committee and pastors led the congregation in the service of worship. It included a procession of flags of nations and states represented in the congregation's membership and Bible and other readings in the several languages of church members. The youth dramatized the story of Pentecost from Acts 2. They concluded by kneeling around the

communion table and praying together in their own first languages. The hymns and special music had been gathered from several national cultures.

8. In the evaluation that followed by the various church groups, many people agreed it was among the most powerful worship experiences they had ever had. And yet twelve people transferred their membership to another congregation because they no longer felt at home in the church they had joined.

In the quick overview of this event one might note a common practice in congregations that intentionally embrace cultural and racial differences. It involves what I call the strategic quest for solidarity. Solidarity is not the same as mutuality. In the experience of mutuality different peoples share similar feelings or ideas. It involves an action of reciprocity, of give and take. The goal of mutuality is to have the sense of belonging to one another—of having empathy for the other. The impetus in groups—including congregations—toward the experience of mutuality is powerful. It originates in our human quest to be connected to others, to share a sense of commitment to one another, to be on intimate terms with another. It draws on the persistent assumption that despite our differences we have something in common.

That sense of belonging integral to mutuality, while possible, is at the same time difficult to achieve in congregations embracing racial and cultural diversity. That difficulty may be traced to a contrary discovery about our human experience. Our differences cannot be reduced to some common denominator. They cannot be merged, blurred, or organized into common categories. So we are male and female, young and old, Gentile and Jew, French and Chinese, Salvadoran and Kenyan, and "black" and "white" and "yellow" and "red." The child born in the 1990s does not see the world in the same way as did her parents at the same age. The symbols, technologies, even language that inform her perceptions provide a different angle on the same events and relationships. In the Bible people whose differences radically distinguished them from others were often called strangers or aliens—those who have not been seen before or are not at home in this place. They are people we do not understand—perhaps may never understand, even after years of living and working together.

Solidarity is the word some contemporary theologians have used to describe the dynamics in communities that affirm and embrace these incomprehensible differences as gifts to our common life. It is based on the assumption that certain facets of our human experience cannot be caught up in consensus, cannot be experienced mutually, cannot be assimilated into the larger life of the congregation or community. When communities or congregations that embrace diversity are in solidarity, their members have not suppressed elements of their cultural (gender, class, etc.) identities. Instead they celebrate the distinctive contributions each person and group brings to their fellowship, worship, and study. Sharon Welch has suggested that in this regard solidarity requires "granting each group" in a congregation "sufficient respect to listen to their ideas" and to be challenged by them.[6]

Conditions for Solidarity

At least four conditions are necessary for developing congregational solidarity. The first involves the creation of times and places for each racial and cultural group in the congregation to meet and talk among themselves. The image Walter Brueggemann develops in a discussion of the 2 Kings 18-19 encounter of the Assyrians and Jews illumines the point. The Jews needed to talk "behind the wall" in their own language within the medium of their own culture before they engaged in the public discussions with the Assyrians at the wall.[7] Strategic solidarity across racial and cultural lines also requires the renewal and intensification of the identification of each group with its own heritage so that its members might bring its wisdom and experience to their place of meeting with others.

The second involves a commitment to take seriously the ideas and experience of others on their own terms—both as individual people and as members of particular racial and cultural groups. This condition is illustrated by the Northwoods Church when its Pentecost liturgy planning committee began its work by asking people to tell their own stories of faith out of the particularity of their cultural and religious experience and to share their own meanings and significance of the Pentecost text before starting to plan the liturgy.

The third condition requires people to suspend their own personal, cultural, and religious ideas and practices to listen for the experience and meanings of others. Although this happened through the planning process, the Pentecost liturgy required it of the entire congregation. A simple example occurred when various people read scripture texts or offered prayers in their own languages. The liturgical bulletin printed all the texts in English and Spanish; even so, everyone still had to suspend personal expectations for how a scripture lesson or prayer would sound. This act of suspending expectations does not involve repressing expectations or holding them in. It is marked by a growing sensitivity to the feeling and tones that lie beneath the speaker's words. For some this act of suspension in the Northwoods liturgy created a greater sense of openness to the movement of the Holy Spirit. For others the experience was so disorienting, they left the worship service saying that if worship would be like this in the future, they would find another church.

The fourth condition involves what Welch calls the "mutuality of critique." In congregations embracing cultural and racial diversity, it seems to take years before people move beyond being concerned about hurting each other's feelings to reciprocal candor about expectations and responsibilities, moral and theological strengths, and blind spots. At Northwoods Church this process began as the pastor became increasingly aware of cultural differences and interpreted them at appropriate times in worship, educational, and administrative settings. It increased as folk talked about what they did not appreciate or honor in the traditions of others. This step can be awkward and difficult. The folk at Northwoods discovered just how difficult when they began to talk publicly about the frustration long-time members felt over the lack of responsiveness of some newer African members to the financial needs of the church. When they finally discussed the matter, they discovered that these new members had always depended on the paternalistic generosity of missionary churches to support the congregations in their homelands. At this point both the paternalism of long-time members and the dependency of some new members on outside help began to be challenged. No quick resolution has yet been found, but the subject is now the topic of mutual conversation and strategic thinking as together members of both cultural groups struggle to find ways to support and extend the congregation's ministries.

Appreciative humor is an important sign of the increasing capacity for mutual critique in the midst of tense encounters. C. A. Bowers has observed that humor often functions as an expression of solidarity in pluralistic settings. When a joke is shared and "breaks the ice" it "signals a shared understanding"—even if for only a moment—and temporarily suspends "dominant and conventionally accepted forms of control." In this process humor alters the power relations in groups and promotes solidarity.[8] It levels the playing field, making possible a different kind of hearing among diverse groups of people. Humor that promotes solidarity does not come easily, because that which people find funny is often very specific to each culture. And yet laughter, and the jokes and stories that prompt it, is frequently heard in the congregations we have visited. Rarely is it planned. Rather it seems to well up out of the cross-cultural confusion and misunderstandings people experience in their relationships, deepening their appreciation for each other.

A chance overhearing of a conversation at Oakhurst added one more dimension to our understanding of Welch's notion of the mutuality of critique. I can no longer remember the issue. But a decision was needed. The woman who was talking recognized that the right response from her perspective could cause some pain for others. There was no time, however, for the kind of careful collaboration we have described elsewhere. So she made the necessary decision and then concluded her comments by saying that she would report it to her friends and request their forgiveness. When asked about this last statement, she replied, "In this church we have to ask each other for forgiveness all the time." Mutual critique, in other words, involves more than a rational intellectual assessment and prioritizing of another's ideas, practices, and moral perspectives to ensure fairness, equity, and justice in congregational life. It culminates in the intensification of the spiritual ties binding one person to another, one group to another.

Culturally and racially diverse congregations practice strategic solidarity in many different ways. Union United Church in Montreal sponsors a Heritage Week each June to celebrate the food, music, art, literature, and religious experience indigenous to its many cultural groups. Northwoods Church sponsors "multicultural events" at different points in the church year to provide opportunities for people to talk to others about the cultural heritage of their religious experience. A recent event on Palm Sunday weekend featured the stories of Lenten observance in three different countries. The practice of sharing joys and concerns at Oakhurst moves beyond the announcement of issues in the lives of church members to include descriptions of the social, cultural, political, economic, and/or theological conditions surrounding the issue. It is a practice that helps people see the reality of others' life experiences and to honor those experiences as the occasion for encountering God's redemptive grace. Each of these activities emphasizes in varying degrees practices integral to the task of nurturing multicultural solidarity. The activities encourage people to get to know one another on their own terms; to listen, suspending temporarily their own cultural preferences and judgments; and to engage others in candid speech that allows for the mutuality of critique.

For Further Reflection

An Exercise to Identify Practices of Strategic Solidarity

Directions:
During a committee meeting or educational event, listen for examples of the four practices described above that indicate effort is being made toward strategic solidarity. If it seems appropriate, you might share what you have heard with other members of the group.

1. Examples of times when people of a particular racial and cultural group meet together and in the process renew and intensify their ties to their own traditions and heritage.

2. Examples of people from different groups listening to one another—illustrating their efforts to hear others on their own terms and out of their own cultural and racial contexts.

3. Examples of people suspending for a time their own preferences, value judgments, or commitments in an effort to understand and appreciate the experience, values, and commitments of someone from a different racial or cultural group.

4. Examples of people from various groups talking about the strengths and problems to be found in their differing cultural and/or racial perspectives on an issue or topic.

An Activity to Implement Insights from this Chapter

A Binding Strategy

The following activity is designed to be used by congregations or groups seeking to deepen or strengthen the ties binding their members into a fellowship of love and care. This activity has been inspired by the research methodologies of my colleagues associated with the Center for Faith Development at Emory University.[9] The ties nurtured through this strategy focus not so much on the interpersonal relationships but more on incorporating newcomers into the congregation's story. This strategy requires a good representation of the membership of the congregation—both long-time and new members, children and youth. It can function as the program for a fellowship dinner or other event involving the total congregation. It can be effectively repeated every three or four years. By that time new people will have entered the fellowship of the congregation—but in my experience, the practice of retrieving and telling stories from the life of the congregation usually reminds people of almost forgotten stories that had a formative influence on how the congregation understands itself and its mission. In the retelling of their stories, congregations have an opportunity to renew their potential to fund their imaginations for their life and mission as well as to challenge the hold that certain events from the past may have on their futures. Here I lay out directions for carrying out this strategy.

1. Supplies needed: a very long sheet of paper (which could include several sheets of newsprint taped together), masking tape to post the paper on the wall, and a handful of magic markers.

2. Hold the meeting in a room with a long blank wall.

3. Post on that wall a sheet of paper that extends as far along the wall as possible.

4. Using a magic marker draw vertical lines to divide the paper into sections. Each column needs enough space to include the information to be listed under each heading. In the first space write the heading "Congregational Memory." In the second space write the dates of the first

decade the member with the longest membership in the church can remember. In each of the following spaces, write the dates of the next decade. So it might look like this:

Congregational Memory	**1920-30**	**1930-40**	**1940-50**	**etc.**

5. As people arrive ask them to write their names in the column of the decade when they moved into the parish or joined the congregation. Ask everyone to use the same color marking pen for this exercise.

6. Ask people baptized in this congregation to write their names into that decade column using a different color.

7. With a third color add the names and the years for the tenure of the pastors and other church staff members.

8. Then ask the whole group to remember key people and significant events that occurred in each decade. Add this information in the appropriate columns. At this point do not spend time talking about who these people were or telling stories to explain what happened. Add information for each decade.

9. After the information has been compiled, go back to the first decade. Ask people to begin to tell stories about some of the people and events listed. Invite people in the group to ask questions about those people and events.

10. If you have time, ask the members of the group to identify any themes or issues they can discern in the stories they have heard. These themes and issues may become the agenda for future discussions in appropriate committees.

11. Leave the tapestry of the congregation's history on the wall for several weeks. You may even provide marking pens so people can continue adding information.

CHAPTER 4

Congregational Conversation

Conversation as a Practice

Shortly after I began visiting the Cedar Grove Church, I overheard a white woman make a suggestion to her pastor. After listening intently, the pastor proclaimed it sounded like a great idea and asked her to discuss it with another woman whom I later discovered happened to be black. In that simple exchange, I discovered a first movement in the practice of conversation of this congregation.

Most of us take this practice for granted. We learn to talk at a very early age. We grow up talking to other people. Talk undergirds the development of our relationships, the quality and character of our education, our ability to gain and sustain employment, our engagement with the political processes in church and public life, and our participation in worship. If we do not talk fluently or hear well, social expectations require us to compensate for whatever limitations we might have. So those of us who are deaf learn sign language and read lips. Others of us who are shy, or like Moses feel inadequate to the task of speaking in public, find ways to communicate through others who are more fluent.

Taking Conversation Seriously

The people in culturally and racially diverse congregations cannot take conversation for granted. The pastor in the congregation described above knew at least subconsciously that centuries of expectations about when and how black and white people talk to each other had to be overcome. Patterns of deference and superiority originating in the relationship of slave and owner and nurtured through centuries of inequities limited the candor central to the talk of brothers and sisters in Christ. Those patterns had to be challenged and unlearned. The people of this congregation had to learn how to talk to one another to give credence to their claims that they were members of a family, members one of another.

Anthropologist Edward Hall has observed that every cultural group develops its own way of talking or interacting within that group.[1] When people move from their own group to another they have to learn the language, as immigrants do when they enter a new country. They have to become familiar with the slang and idiomatic expressions that localize that language. They have to learn how vocal tones and body movements contribute to and reinforce meanings associated with certain words and phrases for the people in that place. And even after years of practice, they may still miss nuances in the vocabulary or behaviors associated with certain patterns of speaking. Such moments reinforce the feelings of being an outsider—one who does not totally belong.

This language barrier can be evident even when one moves from one section of the country to another—and settles among seemingly like folk. I know this from personal experience. I have lived in the southeastern United States for more than sixteen years. My mother grew up in the same region. And yet at times I continue to hear the speech of my neighbors through my Pacific Northwest ears. "A great distance" for me continues to mean a *drive* of at least three or four hours. Note that I think of distance in terms of time. For some of my students "a great distance" may refer to the next county—certainly the next state. Distance for them has more to do with relationships and certain structures of association connected to the place they call home. So to be in Alabama for some Georgians is to be "a great distance" away because there they are no longer surrounded by family and friends.

When we encounter people who do not speak the same language or the same language in the same way we do, the challenge is so great we turn to translators. I remember attending a conference of Christian educators from Japan and the United States. Although most of our Japanese colleagues could read English, few felt comfortable speaking it. None of the U.S. Americans spoke Japanese. We had four translators—two Japanese and two from the United States. We discovered we could talk to each other through the translators, but that in the process our conversation took on a radically new character. Someone would speak. If that person was Japanese, we would wait—suspending our hearing, so to speak—until one of the translators began to translate. Sometimes another of the translators would refine or even correct the first translation. Once in a while all four translators would argue over the meaning of a phrase or word, checking back with the speaker to make sure they had understood correctly, before giving a translation they felt adequate to the speaker's intentions. In the meantime we would continue to wait. Then someone else would speak, and the process would start over. Obviously we covered fewer topics in a given time frame, but after several sessions we found we had developed a rhythmic pattern of speaking and hearing and felt as if we could converse quite easily with one another. We had learned something about the rhythm and structure of conversation mediated through translators. A similar dynamic occurs in any culturally and racially diverse congregation—even those in which a common language is spoken. The various groups in the congregation learn to talk with other groups only as they are in situations where they can practice hearing and speaking to the others.

The *intentional* efforts to hear and speak to each other in the congregation described above made me aware that a similar dynamic is at work in any racially and culturally diverse congregation in which the members have begun to develop deep bonds across groups and to discover that there is no racial or cultural preferential standing before God. At Cedar Grove we discovered that conversation followed a typical pattern. Someone or some group had an idea or concern. Typically he or she would first discuss it with the pastor or one or two lay leaders. Invariably the originator would be told to talk to others–especially of a different gender or racial or cultural group–to discover whether others shared that idea or concern. If the originator found any support for the idea, the discussion would spin out through the congregation. These conversations often occurred after the worship service as people talked on the church grounds. The talk "after church" rarely lasted less than thirty or forty minutes. It occurred while people gathered for fellowship dinners. In this congregation the announced time for a meal was the time when people would arrive to set up for the meal. We observed that the conversation during this time was as important as the meal that followed. People would stay after meetings to talk. There was always time to talk before and/or after any other church-sponsored gathering for the congregation or the larger community. People expected children and youth to overhear these conversations and to join in when they had something to say. Throughout this process the pastor and two or three laypeople monitored the course of the conversation and urged people to extend the discussion in ever wider circles both in the church and the larger community.

The effect of this congregation's approach to conversation altered the way its members conducted church business meetings. During one of the first meetings I attended, someone offered a suggestion for some new program. The subsequent discussion surfaced very diverse opinions about the value of the proposal. Shortly after the disagreements became apparent to everyone present, someone made a motion to table the suggestion. It was immediately seconded and approved by the total group. When I asked the pastor later what had happened, she said that this was a typical way of handling disagreement in committee meetings: Members of the committee would be talking about the proposal with others in the congregation and community during the days and weeks that followed. If through this process the idea or some refinement of it had merit, it would reappear on a future agenda. Typically it would then be approved with little debate. The black and white members of this congregation were not going to trust the future of their fellowship to the power dynamics of majority rule that could easily set new members over against long-time members or white against black members.

Characteristics of Informal Conversation

I have long been fascinated by the ways congregations converse. Some years ago I described the informal conversation of a congregation as the "curricular undercurrent" that sustains and energizes the more formal conversations of liturgy, classroom, and business meeting.[2] When this undercurrent is weak or nonexistent, the structure of the congregation tends to be hierarchical and dependent on clergy leadership. And the bonds that gather the members of the congregation into fellowship tend to be fragile and more susceptible to external influences. In that essay I noted that effective informal conversation of congregations had at least four characteristics. The study of culturally diverse congregations has led me to add two more.

1. Conversations involve speaking and hearing. Conversation develops in the reciprocity of giving and receiving messages. The speaking is energized as long as the participants perceive that they are being "heard"—the messages received have some proximity to the messages they intended to send. Those involved assume the possibility that their thinking, feelings, and/or behavior may be influenced by the content of their conversation and that the quality of their relationship might be intensified. In a diverse congregation this means that when people cross racial and cultural boundaries to talk to someone, they entertain the possibility of suspending the cultural perspectives through which they usually view the topic at hand and through which they make judgments about their relationship to that topic. As previously discussed, this capacity is a crucial element in the nurture of solidarity.

2. Informal conversations occur at the edges or on the margins of the formal life of the congregation. In the example at the beginning of this chapter, these critical conversations occur on the church lawn, while setting up before potluck suppers, before and after meetings, during a chance meeting at the grocery store. Any encounter that leads to conversation may appear to be happenstance, but, for the most part, the talk is intentional. People who want to talk to each other seek each other out. They can often be found in the same place week after week. In this regard conversation takes time. It cannot be hurried—especially when people do not share the same language or cultural traditions. Seemingly recognizing this dynamic at work in conversation, the pastor of the congregation intentionally urged people to engage each other in conversation to discern whether or not they shared a common background. Note that this is also a crucial element in the dynamics of solidarity. Mutuality is not assumed, so common responsibilities become the catalyst to the conversations that develop relationships.

3. Informal conversation is often marked by urgency. People "can't wait" to share something with someone else. This sense of urgency originates not only in a desire to pass along information or to solicit advice from others, but also in the quest to be connected with people who are significant to us. In the racially and culturally diverse congregation, the sense of urgency is enhanced by the fragility of its fellowship. If people do not learn to talk across cultures, the future of the congregation is in doubt. So, again, this pastor's efforts were so unusual because she persisted in turning chance comments to her into discussions among people who would not necessarily have talked with one another—at least beyond the formalities of ritual greetings.

4. Informal conversations create the possibility of transformation. Through conversation people encounter alternative perspectives on an issue or idea; they identify their relationship to it; they may entertain options to prior understandings or beliefs; they may reinforce or alter their commitment to it. Through the transmission of ideas and perspectives, the partners in conversation entertain the possibility of restructuring their sense of reality. They accept the possibility of changing their thinking or feelings about something. This is especially true when conversation crosses the boundaries of race and culture.

To enter into conversation across these boundaries requires enough shared vocabulary to sustain the conversation. When people do not know each other's words, syntax, grammar, or the body language that accompanies a particular cultural group's usage of that vocabulary, they direct their attention to the work involved in communicating. They struggle to listen for something familiar through unfamiliar accents in speech. They struggle for appropriate words to make themselves understood. They wonder if they have been understood. They feel awkward as they stumble over the flow of words and ideas. In the culturally and racially diverse congregation, this experience is common. If conversation is to occur, a common vocabulary must be developed.

Why is worship typically the nerve center of culturally and racially diverse congregations? As I see it, this one setting and this one set of actions nurtures a common vocabulary and practices for congregational conversation. In that shared experience, a vocabulary for informal conversation is being developed. And because it is a scripted conversation (either in the liturgical bulletin or through the repetition of its form), it promotes competence in a form of speech common to all.

5. Effective informal conversation requires "communicative competence" or the capacity to expect to be understood when speaking and to understand when hearing others speak. C. A. Bowers and David J. Flinders have observed that communicative competence ultimately gives people the political capacity to participate fully in the decision-making processes of a group.[3] This hearing and speaking, in other words, empowers their engagement with others and the issues that affect their lives together. In the congregation that embraces racial and cultural diversity, communicative competence requires enough familiarity with the experience of the other to recognize sources to the meanings that every group brings to its discussion of issues and ideas; it also requires enough facility with the congregation's shared vocabulary to take that shared vocabulary for granted. In other words, communicative competence means that people have the capacity to think beyond the words and phrases they use to the meanings as they might be heard by others. This takes practice. Some of the elements in that practice can be found later in this chapter.

6. The conversation of diverse groups is not coercive. Conversation that contributes to congregational solidarity provides enough freedom of space and thought for people to enter into a discussion freely. This freedom does not mean "anything goes." It means that people can practice what Parker Palmer calls the "obedience to truth" from the wisdom of their particular cultural perspectives.[4] This freedom is a crucial characteristic of the multicultural congregation. It establishes the conditions for the affirmation and critique of the contributions of all people in the congregation's conversation. The creation of this free and open space is a challenge for leaders—especially when one racial or cultural group is identified with the congregation's past or when members consistently encounter the dynamics of ethnocentrism at school, at work, or in their neighborhoods.

The creation of a free and open space requires the abandonment of uniform expectations for participation and the affirmation of the possibility of multiple expectations. People do not assume they will enter a relationship or approach a task with shared assumptions. A common example has to do with the different meanings people attach to their relationship to time. I have had to learn that the families of the children I teach in Sunday school have quite different notions of the meaning of time. Few follow the clock in any strict manner. So the class does not begin at 9:15 A.M., as indicated on the schedule in the bulletin. We work instead with the assumption that the class begins for each child as she or he arrives. This requires a team of teachers who can gather a child into the activity in progress and a plan for teaching that has many points of entry throughout the session. In this situation there is no such thing as "arriving early" or "coming late." Time begins when someone arrives. It has not been easy for me to learn to work in the constraints of this approach to time. Obedience to the clock was drilled into me by my parents from a very early age. Friends who share my former allegiance to the sacredness of designated time blocks wonder how I can work in this situation. But I have discovered that the experience of community—

and the conversation that sustains it—need not depend on everyone being present when something starts. Rather, community is experienced through the persistent actions of gathering everyone fully into the embrace of the congregation's life and work before we depart from each other. This does not mean I have abandoned my own culturally embedded values about the meaning of time. I still appreciate the unity of experience that comes when everyone is present for the initial activity of a group. But it does mean I am more comfortable with alternative ways of relating to time. The presence of these options frees up my own relationship to the space in which I interact with others. When they similarly recognize and affirm the diversity of our views of time, we discover together new and deeper ways of communicating.

Informal conversation, grounded in the common vocabulary of liturgy and mission, provides the rhythmic counterpoint in the infrastructure that sustains the education, outreach, fellowship, and worship in culturally and racially diverse congregations. When the conversation is lively and engaging, it nurtures the ties that bind diverse peoples into communal solidarity. It cannot be assumed, however. It must be intentionally nurtured.

For Further Reflection

An Exercise to Discern the Character of Congregational Conversation

Directions:
Review a recent conversation you have had with someone whose racial, cultural, or class heritage differs from your own. What did you say to each other? What were you feeling and thinking during the conversation? What did you each disclose to the other that revealed something of your personal and cultural experience? What relevant information or feelings did you not disclose? Did you feel some reluctance in sharing that information? If so, can you identify why? As you think about this exercise, review the characteristics of informal conversation described above. Which were evident in your interaction with each other? Which were missing? What insights does this exercise suggest for future conversations you might have? For those that occur in the life and work of the congregation?

Empowering Speech

In *The Power to Speak*, Rebecca Chopp quotes Carolyn Heilbrun's definition of power: "the ability to take one's place in whatever discourse is essential to action and the right to have one's part matter." Each phrase reveals an important insight into the dynamics of embracing difference in multicultural congregations. To have "ability" involves more than capacity; it assumes competence. To "take one's place" in the discourse of the congregation requires that one not only has the knowledge and skill for speaking and listening, but also has been accorded the status of one who speaks in and for the congregation. To have one's speech "matter" involves the affirmation that one's speaking (and acting) contributes to and makes a difference in the congregation's common life. Without the "power to speak" on these terms, those with diminished or little privilege, place, or status in the congregation will always be strangers to its life and work.

Chopp goes on to address the experience of women. Her words, however, appropriately describe the experience of some other people in congregations. They will be "forever strangers" to the dominant group in the congregation—whether they be men or some racial, cultural, or socioeconomic group or class—unless their own words and voices help "revise the social and symbolic rules of language" that govern the speech of the congregation; transform the "ordered hierarchy" at work in who gets to speak and whose words have power to influence congregational action; and open up the conversation of the congregation to include the multiplicity of possibilities and perspectives originating from the gendered and cultural locations of the congregation's members.[5]

Empowering speech is a major and persistent task in culturally and racially diverse congregations. Patterns of speech in the larger society permeate the life of the church. So women often defer to men; minority people to people of a dominant cultural group; newcomers to long-time members; children and youth to their elders. Patterns nurtured in interpersonal relationships extend into the public speech of the congregation. In contrast to an earlier era in U.S. and Canadian history, when every school and church event involved a series of public recitations, skits, and speeches by children and youth, only a select few young people today receive any formal training in public speech. This means most remain "speechless" as they move through adolescence into adulthood—at least in the forums where decisions are made. So the task of empowering speech in congregational life involves not only breaking down assumptions about who has the privilege to speak but also providing opportunities for people to develop their capacities for speech. In the next section we explore several strategies that may be employed to empower speech in a congregation with people from different cultures.

For Further Reflection

An Exercise to Identify Empowered Speakers

Directions:
This exercise gathers information on who does and does not speak. It may provide a clue as to who does and does not feel free to speak. The next time you participate in a committee meeting or educational class or program, keep track of the conversation in the following way:

1. Take a sheet of paper.

2. Write the name of everyone present in a column down the left side of the page.

3. Put a tab mark after each person's name every time she or he speaks.

When you have completed the exercise, review the information to identify who may and may not feel empowered to speak. The next sections may provide you with some suggestions about how to create a climate for more empowered speech among the people in the group you surveyed.

Legitimating Speech

I am always intrigued by the reaction of children when they discover that the gospels of Matthew and Luke have different—and at points contrary—versions of the story of the birth of Jesus. "How can that be?" one little boy asked. Behind his question is the prevailing congregational assumption that we as human beings can discern the one right interpretation of a passage of scripture, ascertain the full truth of a statement of faith in a doctrinal proposition, or determine the correct moral response to a life situation. The variety of ways of discerning and knowing truth at work in a culturally diverse congregation dispels this assumption for leaders.

When only one interpretation or practice is allowed, the voices of those for whom other perspectives are important are marginalized. The model is set for us in the Gospels. We have four writers, who often share the same body of narrative material on the life, death, and resurrection of Jesus Christ, but whose telling of that story also reflects values and perspectives originating from their own cultural and religious contexts. A similar dynamic occurs in four distinctive practices to be found in the conversations of many culturally and racially diverse congregations.

Rehearsing Speech

In several multicultural congregations any change in the formal speech of worship, administration, or education is rehearsed as the congregation gathers in a variety of settings through the week. So if a new hymn, litany, or creedal statement is to be introduced in worship, it is first practiced in Sunday school classes, business meetings, youth group meetings, and perhaps during a fellowship meal until the tune and words have become familiar.

If a range of meanings associated with the text for a sermon is to be grasped, people are engaged in conversation around that text in a variety of places. Sunday school and Bible classes focus on the text during the week. Reflections on the text are included in the weekly newsletter. The text may be the subject of discussion at the beginning of a business meeting. Competency in speaking, in other words, is dependent in part on the familiarity of people with the subject of the conversation.

At Northwoods Church rehearsing speech takes a distinctive turn. The Sunday morning liturgy regularly involves more people in leadership roles than I have seen in any other congregation. Besides the two pastors and the traditional role for laity in the choir and as ushers and acolytes, members of the congregation make many of the announcements of events in the life of the congregation. Children, youth, and adults read the Old Testament, Epistle, and Gospel readings. Younger readers usually have practiced their readings for several weeks. If the text lends itself to dramatic presentation, several people may be involved. Several people participate in the leadership of an extended intercessory prayer as the liturgy comes to a close.

Over the years I have observed that members of this congregation are developing a growing fluency with religious language. Their experience contrasts with the general decline of knowledge of religious language in other congregations I know. I suspect this familiarity is due not only to the occasional preparation of people of all ages to read and lead the congregation in worship, but also result from the legitimization of their voices as readers of scripture and petitioners of congregational concerns. These words do not belong to the pastor or preacher; they are the words of the total congregation.

Oakhurst's ritual sharing of joys and concerns provides another example of rehearsing speech that empowers participation—speech that in this case discloses the deepest joys and pains in the experience of congregational members. Empowered speech requires candor on the part of both speaker and hearer. It assumes a safe place to speak that which matters to us. Too often this practice does not extend beyond the naming of that which is in our hearts. I am thinking of congregations in which I have heard people share brief phrases such as, "My sister's sick"; "Let's keep Mrs. Jones in our prayers; her mother died"; "Don't forget to vote this week." Rehearsing speech that empowers requires more revelatory self-disclosure on the part of speakers.

The pastor at Oakhurst establishes a safe place for these moments. For starters, people are given many opportunities to share their joys and concerns each week—in Sunday school and Bible class meetings, at committee meetings, during social gatherings. Second, when people share something, the pastor or another leader asks them to set the concern in context—so that everyone has some sense of the personal, social, political, economic, and theological significance of the situation. The pastor's question broadens the range of issues that people consider to be legitimate concerns to bring to the group. Consequently people speak of the racism they encounter at work or in the political structures of the community, the struggle to decide how to choose which of their employees to dismiss as a part of a corporate downsizing, the anger they feel over the impact of a county zoning commission, the joy of the birth of a baby, and concern about the economic collapse of a Third World country. I have heard them "share" through words and through song. As children and youth express joys and concerns in their own age groups, they develop competence in sharing with adults what is on their minds and hearts. At Oakhurst, as at Northwoods, the repetition of their sharing empowers the speaking of members on a wide variety of issues in the church and other public settings.

Turn Taking

C. A. Bowers and David Flinders call a second conversational practice "turn taking."[6] They have observed that in both informal conversation and the more formal speech patterns of contexts, such as the classroom or a business meeting, the exchange of speech is governed by implicit rules.

The patterns of turn taking in informal conversation may be compared to a tennis game in which speech bounces back and forth from person to person, although language and cultural differences may require negotiation of the way the game is played. When that occurs the situation is often similar to, though usually more refined than, the playground arguments among children about the "right" game rules. Sometimes those differences are worked out. Sometimes the strongest overrule the others. Sometimes people leave, frustrated.

In more formal settings implicit rules of turn taking are governed more by the number of people involved, their role status and authority, and the extent to which certain ways of viewing a given subject or issue are privileged by those who have the most power. The observations of Bowers and Flinders about the classroom are equally relevant for congregations in which the power dynamics function hierarchically or privilege one group over others. Those with more status and power tend to initiate topics, give directions, and provide information more often than those with less status and power. People in less powerful groups tend to limit their speaking to giving answers, acknowledging information, and seeking the right to speak—unless they have decided to "watch" rather than try to enter the conversation. The challenge before leaders in culturally and racially diverse groups and congregations is to level the playing field—to create a space in which speech involves the mutuality of exchange.[7]

Leaders through the years have developed many strategies for turn taking. Brainstorming is one familiar example. It requires that no one speak a second time, until everyone has had an opportunity to comment on the topic at hand. Through his work with multicultural groups, Eric

Law has developed a strategy that he calls "mutual invitation." It is in some ways a variation on brainstorming, with one significant exception. When a person finishes speaking, she invites another person to speak. That person may indicate that he has nothing to say at the moment but will invite someone else to speak. The act of inviting, which to some will seem awkward, has two functions. It affirms the value of a person "independent of that person's verbal ability"—an important issue in multilingual groups. It also recognizes the dynamic in several cultures in which a person does not speak until first addressed by another. This is especially true in cultures in which younger people will not speak in public as a sign of respect for the words of their elders.[8]

The Northwoods Church initiated a strategy of turn taking for general congregational meetings in the midst of a crisis. Shortly after the excitement of the Pentecost Sunday worship had ebbed, the leaders of the Spanish-speaking ministry made the unexpected decision that they wanted to locate in another congregation. Almost immediately after this experience of celebrating diversity, the viability of the vision of becoming "multicultural" was being challenged. After consultation with church leaders and Luther Smith, a professor of church and community at the Candler School of Theology, the pastor invited all who would to attend a meeting to consider prayerfully the future of the congregation. The process he suggested was quite straightforward. Out of his consultation with several people, he had chosen several passages of scripture that had the potential to speak to various aspects of the crisis they now experienced.

When people arrived they discovered the chairs in a very large circle in the fellowship hall. A good cross section of the members of the church showed up. The pastor described in detail the situation in which the church now found itself. He then outlined the process for the rest of their time together. He would read a passage of scripture. As people listened, they were to seek to discern God speaking to the congregation through those words. After several minutes of meditative silence to listen to what those words were saying to them individually, the pastor asked those present what they had heard. He requested that no one comment on the thoughts of others. The purpose of the meeting was to listen. It was not to discuss what each person had heard. Each comment was duly written on newsprint to be compiled for discussion in other group meetings at other times. No one in the group had participated in this kind of meeting before. The ground rules for contributing were new. Although some felt constrained by these rules, they shifted the traditional power dynamics in the conversations of the congregation and may have contributed to the full participation of those present. After everyone had the opportunity to speak, the pastor turned to the second, then the third reading. Time ran out before he could complete the fourth and fifth. Upon their arrival, people had talked in tones of discouragement. When they left, they spoke with hope for the future. No vote was taken, but the mood of the place indicated that few, if any, doubted that the congregation's future continued to exist in its multicultural vision. That mood, I would suggest, may be traced in part to the decision to enter into the conversation with a clearly defined strategy of turn taking to ensure the contribution of all.

Open Scripting

A third practice for legitimating the speaking of diverse voices might be described as writing an open-ended script. It involves providing explicit opportunities for different groups to contribute to the public and formal speech of the congregation in ways that honor their traditions, experience, and perceptions. An example may be seen in the approach taken by Oakhurst Church as its members prepare for the annual Christmas pageant. Although the form varies somewhat from year to year, several elements in the preparations are consistent. The pageant draws on three seasonal traditions. The year I participated, the evening began with a potluck supper and a ritual organized around the themes of Kwanza. It continued with the traditional North American Christmas pageant but reshaped on the traditions of the Mexican posada—a ritual quest for the birthplace of the Christ child. Three distinct traditions are celebrated interdependently honoring the experience in each and yet drawing on the resources of each for a distinctively Oakhurst Christmas celebration. This establishes the context for the strategy of open scripting through which the posada or pageant is prepared.

Thematic moments in the script of the posada or pageant are assigned to Sunday school classes of all ages and various congregational groups—the Annunciation, the journey from Nazareth to Bethlehem, the census, the quest for a place to stay, and so forth. Each group is responsible for developing the costumes, the actions, and in many instances the speech of the assigned scenes. No one knows for sure what will be done or said outside of his or her own group until it happens. The perspective on each segment in the production is shaped by the age, experience, and cultural viewpoint of those who created it. All who contribute to the creation of the *script* participate in the event. The collaborative effort of all participants becomes speech through which the congregation encounters the gospel of the Incarnation. People of all ages and cultural backgrounds become, in the process, contributors to the public speaking in the congregation.

The Advent and Christmas seasons provide only one of the more familiar opportunities for practices of open scripting. Any event or circumstance can be an effective occasion for the practice. I have seen and heard youth present a skit as the "sermon" on the challenges of growing up adolescent in today's world. I have also seen youth planning the liturgy and preparing the sermon, children producing plays, and people of all ages working on skits for fellowship dinners or promoting a missional activity.

In the scripts prepared for each of these activities, the words (and the cultural images and meanings behind them) of the various groups become a part of the congregation's public conversation. The voices of diverse groups are in this way recognized and valued for their contributions to the life and work of the congregation.

Making the Ground Rules for Communication Explicit

One of the most important functions of leaders in multicultural congregations is to make explicit the ground rules for the formal conversations of committee meetings, educational experiences, even liturgical and social events. On the surface this seems like a relatively easy thing to do. Making ground rules explicit, however, challenges those implicit ground rules that support and reinforce social conventions upholding the structures of hierarchy, privilege, and status and the structures that sustain the dynamics of racism and ethnocentrism.

Explicit rules for communication can effectively challenge "ways we have always done things." To illustrate I contrast what I observed in Cedar Grove with what I saw in several other racially and culturally diverse congregations. Like Cedar Grove these churches in committee meetings acted to dismiss proposals or projects that evoked any significant criticism. But unlike Cedar Grove, here I sensed no ground rules governing the continuation of those conversations outside the context of a committee. So the proposal would die without any rigorous review. Some congregational decisions to "table" proposals are in effect only slightly veiled actions to perpetuate the power of the dominant group. When the members of that group are European Americans, the decision, for all practical purposes, serves to perpetuate the experience of margination of minority groups and extend the structures of racism.

When congregations make explicit guidelines to ensure the participation of all groups in their discussions, they seek not only to legitimate the speech of all, but also to transform any conventions that served to promote the interests of one group over another. Any consideration of guidelines for empowered conversation should articulate the following:

1. A clear description of the purposes for the gathering.

2. A description of the ground rules for conversation; for example, *Robert's Rules of Order* or the invitational method proposed by Eric Law.

3. Instructions on how topics will be proposed and decisions will be made.

4. The importance of taking time to build interpersonal relationships; to share stories of personal and cultural experiences related to the topic or issue under discussion; to share joys and concerns of group members since they last met together; to engage in a Bible study on a relevant theme to discover the relationship of group members to the text's ideas, themes, and experiences; to identify what each person brings in terms of background, knowledge, experience for the topic of discussion; and so forth.

5. An evaluation process that focuses as much on how people felt about the way discussions were conducted and decisions were made as on the product or outcome of the session.[9]

For Further Reflection

Exercises to Discern Practices in Legitimating Speech

Exercise 1

Directions:
During another meeting or educational event, *assess* the kinds of speaking people do. People who feel their speech is legitimated by the group tend to make contributions that empower the group process. They initiate topics, ask questions, give directions or instructions, and share information. To find out to what extent the tasks are shared by the various members of the group and by people of different racial and cultural groups, create the following guide for listening to the group's conversation. During the meeting put a check mark in the appropriate column after each person speaks.

1. Take a sheet of paper.

2. Write the names of all people who are present down the left side of the paper.

3. Make four columns with the following headings:

Initiates Topics	Asks Questions	Gives Directions	Shares Information

Exercise 2

Directions:
Review the information you have collected in the previous two exercises. Explore the extent to which you think your findings may reflect the larger conversations of the congregation. What steps do you need to take to ensure greater and wider participation of individual people and groups in the conversation of your congregation?

Accepting Ambiguity

One Sunday morning at Cedar Grove Church, when we came to that point in the order of worship in which the pastor calls the congregation into prayers of confession, she asked people to stand. She then described the anger, frustration, and tension that had filled many of the conversations of church members during the past week or two. She asked people to move through the sanctuary, look each other in the eyes, and say, "In the name of Jesus Christ, you are forgiven." I have already written about a woman who had made a similar statement at the Oakhurst Church.

These two actions reveal an important feature in the lives of culturally and racially diverse congregations. Conversation has limits. It can never nurture the depth of understanding or the intensity of mutuality that we seek in our meetings with others. It is never adequate to the task of communicating the fullness of our experience of the gospel or the pain we have known. Cultural differences of perspective and practice are too deeply embedded in our sociocultural experience. The point was made by the pastor of Northwoods Church after several years of leading Bible study groups that included people from several different national cultures from every region of the globe. "I can look in their eyes after a statement about a particular passage of scripture," he observed, "and see that the only ones whose hearing may approximate my intended message are those who share my southern white heritage. White folks from other parts of the country catch on pretty quick, but there are times when I know that some people hear something radically different from my intentions."

I have heard several people describe the differences in the way many white and black Christians from the United States talk about Moses. A common black Christian perspective views Moses as the liberator of the Israelites from slavery; a more common white Christian perspective emphasizes the role of Moses as the giver of the law. When embedded in the meaning systems of their respective cultures, these two angles of vision on the work of Moses function as a lens through which other experiences and relationships may be interpreted. The reaction of my students from a variety of racial and cultural backgrounds to an essay on the Exodus by Robert Allen Warrior, a member of the Osage Nation of Indian Tribes, illustrates that as the number of cultural groups increases in a congregation, the possibilities for interpretation and meaning become more complex. After reflecting briefly on the African-American engagement with that ancient narrative, Warrior writes that "The obvious characters in the story for Native Americans to identify with are the Canaanites, the people who already lived in the promised land." What does it mean, he wonders, to look at a text about the liberated from the vantage point of those who were colonized?[10]

In a racially and culturally diverse congregation, these three (and more) perspectives on this ancient story could be present in a Bible study group. On the one hand, they can enrich the conversation. On the other hand, when examined closely, the views represent three radically alternative meaning perspectives. Those who viewed Moses as the lawgiver have been agents of the law. Those who viewed Moses as liberator have known centuries of slavery and oppression. Those who viewed the Israelites as conquerors have themselves been conquered and many have been banished from their homelands. In some respects these differences of interpretation are not just cultural perspectives on that ancient story; they embody incommensurably different ways of relating to it and to those who hold alternative perspectives.

Incommensurability is a big word. I have tried to find a simpler one to make the point that oil and water cannot be made to mix unless their properties have been changed in some significant way. Both oil and water have integrity. Together they provide the resources for something new. So do the interpretations grounded in our various cultural ways of seeing things. Leaders of multicultural congregations regularly bump up against incommensurable differences of experience and perspective. I am reminded of a liturgy-planning committee meeting. In this congregation a different group of laypeople is asked each season of the church year to help choose the hymns and the general prayers for the weekly liturgy. This is a task taken very seriously. A person is asked to prepare for a specific Sunday. He or she is given the lectionary readings and a hymnal to peruse. The "season's group" then comes to a meeting and coordinates the schedule. A planning group consists of members of all ages, male and female, and from several different national and cultural groups. The ensuing conversation over texts, tunes, and the intent of scripture passages for the day and season often runs deep. It has become a powerful context for theological learning.

Shortly after one particular group started on its task, the discussion turned to some hymns chosen for the previous liturgical season. The congregation had sung the Lord's Prayer to a calypso tune found in the denominational hymnal. An older European American who had been squirming in her seat finally announced that she had been talking with a number of friends (all European American) in her women's circle and Sunday school class. "Everyone," she underscored, agreed with her feelings about that hymn tune. It was "offensive." It did not "seem right" to pray the Lord's Prayer to a dance tune. It soon became clear that this was not just a difference of opinion about music because for her, and the people for whom she spoke, the music radically altered the sacredness of the prayer, and with it the way she stood before God. She concluded by saying that she knew others disagreed with her, but she "just could not worship when that tune was used to sing the Lord's Prayer."

The next person to speak was from Jamaica. She said she had grown up singing the Lord's Prayer to that tune; that it was associated in her mind with some of the most significant moments of prayer in her life; that it reconnected her to the faithfulness of important teachers and mentors. The impasse between these two perspectives could not be resolved during that meeting. This congregation had officially declared itself to be a "multicultural church." From that perspective, if the journeys of faith of these two women were to be honored, their differences had to be respected. And so the discussion concluded with each woman expressing to the other her willingness to acknowledge the other's viewpoint, but this acknowledgment did not change their convictions. When I have relayed this scenario in workshops and in my classes, someone always wants to know how the situation was resolved. I have to say that it has not been. They both continue to worship together in the same church. They do so, however, knowing that at some point their incommensurable feelings about that hymn tune will once again be put to the test.

How can congregations be responsive to the range of cultural perspectives in their worship, education, and fellowship? The challenge is a big one. And yet many congregations seem to be discovering ways to live with the ambiguity that occurs when cultural differences are embraced. Perhaps David Augsberger has a clue to the dynamic at work in these congregations. People in multicultural congregations may be willing and able to move beyond empathic efforts to understand those of another culture. With empathy people share common cultural assumptions, values, and patterns of thinking. Moving beyond empathy involves developing the sensibilities of what Augsberger calls "interpathy," the quest to envision the thoughts and feelings of a totally separate "other" who does not share my cultural assumptions, values, and views. But with interpathy even that effort is less than what the other perceives and experiences.[11] More than once I have heard members of a multicultural congregation remark that from this gap—between their attempts to see the world through another person's experience and that person's actual experience—they most expect to be surprised by the work of the Holy Spirit. This attitude suggests that ambiguity is not to be feared or distrusted. Rather it is the context for new and deeper encounters with the mystery of God. So how do multicultural congregations embrace the ambiguity that emerges from the encounter of their cultural perspectives? Several leadership tasks seem to be consistently present. They include:

1. Creating a safe place for people to share personal and group perspectives, values, and commitments without fear of judgment.

2. Expanding the number of voices in the conversation and the range of their views on the subject under discussion.

3. Practicing ways of singing, praying, speaking, envisioning, and serving indigenous to several cultures to the point they become a part of their own faith habits.

4. Creating opportunities for people to guide others into their cultural experience of worship, study, care for others.

5. Suspending the desire for cultural coherence in ministry activities. A liturgy can contain music by Palestrina and from the folk traditions of various cultures.

6. Offering occasions for people to request and to offer forgiveness for misunderstandings and mutual hurt.

For Further Reflection

Exercise to Discern Patterns of Accepting Ambiguity

Directions:
During the next meeting or educational setting in which you find yourself, keep a list of the viewpoints of each person who speaks. After the meeting review the list. Was more than one perspective on a topic offered? Did the conversation move so as to reject or ignore the views of people from certain cultural groups? Did the conversation flow in such a way as to explore possibilities in quite divergent points of view? Were the members of the group energized by the multiple perspectives offered in the discussion, or did they find them frustrating? As you think about your answers to these questions, to what extent do you think the group is able to accept the ambiguity that arises from the multiple perspectives of the people who participated?

An Activity to Implement Insights from this Chapter

A Conversational Strategy

The following activity is designed to build on the discussion of this chapter. It is an adaptation of the listening and turn-taking strategy used by Northwoods. It contains two basic movements. The first gathers information. The second lifts up what Paulo Freire called "generative themes"—themes or issues that generate a shared commitment to further study and action. These two movements may be included in a long session or divided into two sessions. Following are instructions for implementing that conversational pattern:

1. Determine the topic or issue to be discussed.

2. Publicize the event. Even more important, people preparing for the conversation need to personally invite others to participate.

3. Arrange the chairs in a circle in the meeting room. Have a large blackboard or plenty of newsprint posted at one end of the circle where all can see.

4. If there is any chance people may not know or remember the names

of everyone present, have name tags ready for people to fill out in large letters.

5. The leader should announce the purpose of the meeting, identify the time for adjournment, and invite the group to pray for God's guidance and blessing.

6. The leader should then describe the ground rules for the conversation. Typically ground rules describe the structure and process for the conversation.

Part 1: Gathering Information

1. The leader clearly and succinctly describes the issue or concern to be discussed.

2. The leader summarizes briefly the reasons why it has been brought to this group for discussion.

3. The leader reads a brief selection of scripture that has the potential to illumine the issue.

4. The group sits in silence for three to five minutes; the leader asks participants to listen carefully for what God might be saying to them through their hearing of the words of scripture regarding the issue or concern being discussed. Their listening might be guided by questions such as "What is God's calling for us in this situation?" or "What are the signs of our responsiveness to God's calling?" or "How do we (or can we) acknowledge and celebrate the vitality of the Spirit in this situation?"

5. The leader asks group members to share the thoughts and insights they "heard" during the moments of silence. Plenty of time needs to be given so that anyone who wishes to speak may do so. This may mean pauses and moments of silence in the process.

6. The leader asks someone to list these ideas and thoughts on the blackboard or newsprint.

7. The group *is not* to discuss any idea or thought suggested at this point. This may be the most important guideline of all. A discussion of topics reintroduces the power dynamics typically associated with formal conversation in the congregation. The purpose of this strategy is to hear the thoughts of as many people as possible.

8. After everyone has expressed thoughts from the first reading and period of silence, the leader may read the second reading and go through the process again.

Part 2: Generating Themes for Discussion

1. The leader asks the group to look over the list of statements written on the blackboard and to identify themes and issues that the group agrees need to be explored or developed further. (If this is a second meeting, this step can take the form of a review of the information listed on the newsprint or blackboard.)

2. The leader then divides the group into smaller groups and gives each group a theme or issue. The leader asks the group to identify who is affected by the theme or issue; how they are affected by it; and why it is important for a Christian community to take this theme or issue seriously. The group should also identify other information it needs to address the theme or issue fully.

3. Each small group then reports its conversation to the larger group. The larger group should ask questions of clarification and interpretation.

4. The leader leads the group in identifying the most important themes and issues for future work.

5. The leader asks people to take responsibility for developing these themes and issues for future discussions.

Closure

1. The leader announces future meeting times and places.

2. The leader thanks people for participating and invites them to hold hands for prayers of thanksgiving and sending out.

CHAPTER 5

Congregational Events

In this chapter we turn to the practices that form and shape—give order to—multicultural congregations. At one level these issues are similar to those faced in any congregation. As Lovett Weems has suggested, these fundamental issues include attention to the development of an empowering vision to guide congregational ministries, a team capable of giving leadership to those ministries, a culture to sustain congregational life, and practices to nurture values and virtues.[1]

The embracing of racial and cultural difference introduces a new element into the discussion of these issues. A major theme of this book has been that with the embrace of diversity, pastors and lay leaders, primarily through trial and error, have discovered that they must attend to the infrastructure of their congregations—those images, relational ties, and patterns of conversation that cross the boundaries of race and culture. The following story may set a framework for this discussion.

The Ordering of Congregational Practices

During a visit to the East Harlem Protestant Parish back in the mid-1960s, I began to understand the concept of liturgy as the *work* of the people. I had heard in my seminary worship class that the origins of the word *liturgy* could be traced back to a combination of the ancient Greek *leiter* or *work* and *laos* or *people* and meant "something performed for the benefit of the city." Early church leaders used it to refer to "something performed by the people for the benefit of others." In other words, all who participated in the work benefited from it.[2] This notion, when applied to the work of worship, was new to me. I had rather naively viewed worship as something like a meal in a restaurant. If the worship leaders, who might be compared to the chef, host, hostess, and servers, did their work well, we "feasted." If their effort was more routine, we might be filled and satisfied. If their work was sloppy or inattentive, we might leave hungry or frustrated.

On that Sunday morning at East Harlem Parish, with a ministry that crossed the borders of race, class, and culture, I had a different experience. Worship was more like a church potluck supper.[3] Everyone contributed; everyone participated; everyone benefited. When we arrived, people at the door greeted us even as they busily folded and stuffed bulletins. As we walked into the sanctuary, someone played the piano. The hymn tunes being rehearsed were the ones we would later sing. Choir members arrived one by one and took their place near the piano. The piano player-choir director ran the singers through a couple of warm-up exercises, then turned to us in the congregation and asked us to practice with the choir a "new" hymn to be sung later as a part of worship. At this point we were also pulled into the work. We did not simply sing through the hymn once, as I had done in some other churches. We rehearsed the words and rhythm, until the director was satisfied with how we sounded. While all of this was going on, people continued to come by to greet and welcome us as they attended to various tasks around the room. Almost everyone—of a wide variety of ages—seemed to have some responsibility. Their focused activity filled the air with anticipation. The feeling resembled that which surrounds the bustle of preparation for a church fellowship dinner or the opening night for a community-sponsored dramatic production. The choir director brought the rehearsal of music to a close. The prelude began. The mood changed. We were no longer preparing and practicing. Everything was now ready. Our work was now focused in worship.

We later learned that the anticipation we felt had been nurtured earlier in the week in Bible study groups as members grappled with the sermon text and what it meant for their lives. Those discussions helped ground the preacher's work in the work of that community. A report during the worship service by people who had gone to City Hall to protest a proposed housing policy intensified our awareness of the connections they made between the work in this place and the work of daily living. On that visit I became aware of worship as the work of the congregation. And I now see that in the way the people of this parish worked together, we were also introduced to a distinctive way of shaping the experience of the people who participated in its life and mission.

The shaping or ordering of congregational life is more complicated than most of us realize. Goals must be set, gifts distributed, relationships nurtured, stories told, decisions implemented, tensions and conflicts negotiated. Even in the smallest of congregations, Larry Rasmussen has observed, congregational life includes "roles and rituals, laws and agreements"—indeed "the whole assortment of shared commitments and institutional arrangements that order the common life." Those arrangements have to do with who gets to speak, to whom and when, how decisions are made, how time will be organized, what accounts of the stories of the community's life will be told, and how differences will be viewed and engaged. They hold communities together—including congregations—against their predisposition to fall apart. They encourage mutual accountability in maintaining and renewing certain beliefs, values, and practices. The ordering or shaping of the life of a community, Rasmussen continues, is "the practice that provides the choreography" for all its other practices.[4]

In *Educating Congregations*, I described how the practice of ordering congregational life often involves the interplay of two quite different choreographic assumptions and styles. One has a programmatic perspective and structure; the other is oriented around significant events.[5] Most workshops and seminars on leadership and congregational management focus on programmatic skills and approaches to ordering congregational life. Let's discuss this typical approach and then move on to the alternative I saw in East Harlem and in many multicultural churches I have visited over the years.

Programmatic Practices

Programmatic practices emphasize the development of options in the ministry of congregations; efforts to order or shape the life of the congregation require coherent objectives and clear criteria for prioritizing and scheduling events to be performed, a plan of activities to be completed. Elected or appointed leaders guide these processes of planning, decision making, and coordination. They recruit, train, and supervise people who implement and publicize those plans to attract the participation of still more people. Efficiency, order, and publicity are primary values. Innovation and responsiveness to new circumstances are important strengths.

In my experience congregations may approach the task of developing and implementing programmatic ministries in a number of ways. Some first develop a mission statement to establish a platform or framework for planning. Other congregations coordinate the activities of their various groups into a common calendar. In either case options are given for the participation of the members of the congregation. As soon as one set of options concludes, another is offered. People choose whether or not to participate. Continuity of purposes, methods, and values occurs implicitly rather than explicitly. Each programmatic activity could stand on its own. People in congregations are rarely given theological or ethical guidelines to help choose among the available program options. Instead marketing techniques similar to those used by the various shops in a shopping mall publicize the activity to attract the participation of people. Although significant ministry does happen through programmatic practices for ordering congregational life, the values embedded in these practices are often more like those of entertainment than of mission.

Event-Centered Practices

When I began to visit black and multicultural churches with some regularity, I slowly recognized the features of an alternative approach to ordering congregational life and ministry. With the help of Robert MacAfee Brown, I came to call this approach event-centered. In *Is Faith Obsolete?* he observed that Christian faith "stands in a special relationship to the past." Something happened that evokes a response in people through time.[6] The meanings associated with the event that happened must be put to some use. Those meanings are conveyed through time in the stories people tell about what happened, through the interpretations people make of the stories they tell, in the ritual practices they develop to embody and reenact the meanings identified with that event, and through authorities that determine which versions, which doctrines, which practices are to be accepted as authentic or correct. An event in this sense is more than a happening in time; it is a theological category for experience that breaks through our sense of chronological time.

From this perspective, faith-prompting events in the past are not confined to the past. They are renewed and lived whenever the stories told, the rituals enacted, and new interpretation made make claims on the lives of individual people and their communities. I first became aware of the ways in which events live through time into the present in a black-congregation worship service. In the middle of the sermon, I realized that this congregation was for all practical purposes *in Egypt* and slowly and laboriously working its way to the Promised Land. The urban landscape did not look like Sinai. The names and faces of those in power were different, but through the telling of that story they were living in that event. Then I saw with a new sense of vision that, for many people, participation in the Eucharist on Maundy Thursday was not a reenactment of the Last Supper but involvement in the unfolding of that fateful meal; for some, attendance in a Good Friday service provided not only an occasion for remembering the story of that day, but also a reliving of the crucifixion event; for others, visiting prisoners is not only a Christian duty, but also the path of discipleship.

Meanings associated with certain events in the past, in other words, become normative for us when we begin to order our lives around them. We define who we are in relation to them. When we take on their perspective, they give us a certain form and shape. In the ordering of congregational life, I discovered that this process involves at least four movements: (1) *preparing* people to participate in the primary stories and rituals of the event(s) that define who they are as a Christian community of faith; (2) *creating occasions for people to participate* in the stories, rituals, and acts of interpreting the meanings associated with those events; (3) *remembering* together the power and significance of those events for their personal and corporate lives; and (4) *making decisions* to extend the influence of the meanings of those events in the ministries of the congregation. These four movements establish the tasks and the rhythmic structure of the management and leadership of event-centered congregations.

In *Educating Congregations*, I observed that four kinds of events help establish the shape of the life and mission of congregations. I have called them paradigmatic, seasonal, occasional, and spontaneous events. These words provide clues to their place and function in congregational ministries.

Paradigmatic events establish the paradigm or pattern for the way a congregation orders its life. For Christians the central paradigmatic event or pattern is usually the life, death, and resurrection of Jesus Christ. The stories of this event give meaning to congregational activities and nurture hope for the congregation's future. Through the centuries the stories of this event have taken many forms—as seen in the four variations in the accounts of Matthew, Mark, Luke, and John, in the doctrinal standpoints and communal practices of various Christian denominations, in the range of sociocultural experiences of that story, and in the local versions found in the life and faith habits of individual congregations. This paradigmatic event typically establishes the framework of meaning for the visions congregations have for the future of their ministries.[7]

Our participation in the narrative structure of these paradigmatic events occurs through a series of *seasonal events* that gather us up into repeated activities of telling and retelling, interpreting and reinterpreting, embodying and reenacting the stories associated with them. In the church the repetition of these seasonal events establishes, among other things, a liturgical calendar of festival days and periods of preparation. So we move through the days of Advent in ways that are similar to the preparations we make for a birthday party, anticipating all the while the Christmas Day celebration of the Incarnation. Through the season of Epiphany, we rehearse the stories of the life and ministry of Jesus. Then we move into another season, Lent, preparing us for reliving the trauma of Holy Week and the celebrative victory of Easter. And the year progresses through the celebration of the resurrection of Jesus, the birth of the church at Pentecost, and the challenges of learning to live into the eschatological future. The movement of the congregation through the stories integral to these seasonal events is intensified by weekly gatherings into rituals through which people encounter their most powerful symbols.

The liturgical calendar does not mark the only seasonal congregational events. Some congregations emphasize the interplay of paradigmatic Christian stories with local cultural stories focused around events such as Homecoming Sunday, Thanksgiving, the Christmas bazaar, the annual revival, the fall barbecue, a festival honoring the parish saint, and Mother's Day.

Whether liturgical or nonliturgical, these events order and move the life of the community through the year. Everyone participates; everyone benefits. So on Christmas and Easter, as well as on Homecoming Sunday or the celebration of the parish saint's day, people who have left the congregation and those who relate to it only marginally return to hear once again a story that gives meaning and hope to their lives.

Occasional events, such as the celebration of a baptism, a wedding, a funeral, a church dedication, or a special mission project, provide other occasions for telling other kinds of stories integral to the paradigmatic gospel story that gives the congregation its reason for being.

And *spontaneous events* surprise congregations with unexpected opportunities to rehearse and renew its participation in the meanings of ancient events and their stories. Such events might include the challenge of deciding what to do with an unexpected financial bequest, how to commemorate the death of a deeply loved member, or how to respond to the destruction of the church building by fire.

Characteristics of Event-Centered Congregations

Event and programmatic practices for ordering the life of communities usually coexist in most contemporary congregations in North America. At times—for instance, with the celebration of Christmas, Easter, the annual revival, the parish saint's day, or Mother's Day, or, as in East Harlem, the weekly gathering of the congregation into worship—event strategies dominate the imagination and energy of congregational members. At other times—as in the organization of educational classes, stewardship campaigns, recreational and social activities, and mission projects—programmatic practices predominate. Programmatic practices tend to dominate the imagination of congregations with enough resources to support highly trained professional staff members who can create and coordinate program options to serve the varied interests and concerns of their members. Event-centered practices tend to predominate in congregations in liturgical denominations, in congregations that emphasize the importance of interpersonal and community ties, in congregations with limited resources, and in congregations that embrace racial and cultural differences. This preference for event-centered practices for ordering the ministries of these congregations may be traced to some of their distinctive characteristics, as described below.

Creating Community

Programmatic practices usually begin with the assumption that the congregation exists within a taken-for-granted cultural ethos. Attention is given to helping people become acquainted with one another in groups designed for specific ages, interests, or abilities. But few people think through the challenge of what it means to develop programs that might create a sense of community that cuts across the deeply rooted boundaries of race, culture, class, and ability.

By way of contrast, event-centered practices emphasize the creation of community. Because events attract diverse groups of people, attention is given to ways of enhancing the participation of everyone. This includes the development of a common vocabulary through which people might comfortably interact as they participate together in shared events and familiar rituals.

The pattern of reenacting the gospel story at Northwoods Church may be illustrative of the development of a common vocabulary. The congregation orders its life around the lectionary. That is not the only way of ordering congregational life around the gospel story, but for this congregation it provides a sustained and deliberate structure for engaging that story. Note the contexts for the telling of the story in this congregation. A different liturgy committee meets for each church season, working through the texts to choose hymns and other liturgical responses appropriate to the season. As of late the pastor sends the lectionary readings for each Sunday to some members by e-mail to elicit their suggestions for his sermon. The choir director and acolyte coordinator provide a continuing commentary on the relationship of their tasks to the meaning of the events for which they are preparing. The Sunday school classes for children and youth use a lectionary-based curriculum. Teachers structure each session so that children encounter at least one of the day's texts at least three times during the Sunday school hour. They usually read the story, do some art project around the story, and often dramatize the story in some way. The children and youth all attend the worship service that follows, and there they again hear the readings, read by different lay members. The youth minister tells a story, often based on the same text. The sermon engages the congregation in a close examination of the text. This congregation assumes that this unified effort is needed if the diverse groups in its membership are to experience the power of *corporate* worship and be moved to participate in a *common* ministry.

I have already described several rituals for creating the ties that nurture a sense of community in diverse congregations: the ritual of greeting and the practice of sharing joys and concerns whenever folk get together at Oakhurst; the linking of people who did not know each other in a Chicago congregation. The point these congregations make is that relationships cannot be assumed. They must be nurtured intentionally every time people get together.

Facilitating Participation

This last comment leads to a second characteristic of event-centered practices for ordering congregational life: They focus more attention on relational dynamics than on organizational procedures and principles. This preference is clearly seen as one contrasts programmatic and event-centered approaches to preparing for events or activities. Event-centered practices emphasize participation in the *preparation* of an event; programmatic practices emphasize the *production* of an activity or event that itself will draw participants. Event practices tend to blur the lines about who can and cannot participate. Programmatic practices tend to target specific *audiences*.

Participation in congregational programs tends to be voluntary, in the sense that they require extensive publicity on the part of planning committees to recruit participants. Participation in events, on the other hand, tends to be assumed—as central to the identity and vocation of the congregation. It is what people do who participate in the life of this congregation. This may seem to contradict the above observation that programmatic approaches assume the presence of an ethos from which people are drawn to participate in planned activities, whereas event-centered approaches assume that the congregational ethos must be created. Actually my point here only reinforces that previous observation. In event-centered practices of ordering congregational life, many people are gathered into the preparation of the events in which they will later participate because this is the process through which the community is formed.

The distinction between event practices and what one pastor has called "institutional" approaches to ordering ministry may also be discerned in the sources of the rhythmic patterns in congregational life. Programmatic approaches establish internal rhythms based on clear beginnings and endings. A mission program begins on Sunday and continues each week for three months. A Bible study runs for six weeks. A retreat begins on Friday night and ends at Sunday noon. The focus on beginnings and endings makes explicit the time commitments expected of participants and the structures of relationship among church members. People associate with certain people for certain times. In large congregations that may be the only time they ever meet.

Although event-centered practices also have timetables of beginnings and endings, their expectations of commitments tend to be more open-ended and relational. I have already illustrated the process in the descriptions of the preparation of Oakhurst's Christmas Eve pageant and Northwoods' Pentecost service. Another example may be seen in an annual mission activity at Northwoods. For many years the congregation has given active support to a walk-a-thon for a denominational community mission agency. Two people typically serve as the coordinators of the event. In a recent year as this team planned for the event, they informally talked about their ideas with people in different Sunday school classes and groups. Several people in the adult Sunday school classes took it upon themselves to promote the activity in those groups. Someone suggested that a T-shirt be created, and several people who thought that would be a good idea designed and ordered them. Teachers asked children to draw outlines of their shoes, which they then cut out and posted in a long line down the hallways with hand-made signs urging people to sign up for the walk. The coordinators talked about the activity during the announcements of the congregation and wrote articles for the weekly newsletter. People told stories about the walks in previous years and informally challenged themselves this year to get more people involved and more money raised. They wore their T-shirts to various church activities. People who could not walk contributed money, sponsoring walkers who ranged in age from seven to over eighty. Adults volunteered to be "parents for a day" for "walker" children whose parents had to work or could not otherwise participate. There was no way that someone in the congregation could be detached from the engagement of people in this event. The leaders of the event established a basic framework for the participation of people and then supported the initiatives of people throughout the congregation who became excited about some task related to it. These activities did more than support the project. They built bridges among people of different ages and backgrounds. They nurtured mutuality and helped to deepen friendships across racial and cultural lines. And they *gathered* as many people as possible into some facet of the activity.

Celebrating Multiplicity

Programmatic practices for ordering congregational life emphasize efficiency and control. Decisions are made in an orderly fashion. Responsibilities are delegated. Authority is clearly designated. By way of contrast, event-centered practices more highly value participation, spontaneity, and variety. The contrast may be seen in two kinds of dinner parties. Those guided by programmatic values are like a formal dinner. The host(ess) is in charge, chooses whom to invite, sends out invitations, selects the menu and often the recipes, sets the table, choreographs the conversation, and oversees every phase of the occasion. Many people may help implement the plans of the host(ess), but they do not alter the basic plan. Guests who come enjoy the hospitality and the creativity of the hostess.

A dinner party influenced by event-centered practices will be quite different. The host(ess) may invite several people to dinner. While talking to a potential guest, the host(ess) discovers that the woman's parents are visiting and encourages them to come. Another person responds to the invitation by asking if he might bring something. After some discussion they agree he will bring a salad. Another guest volunteers to bring dessert. When people arrive for the dinner party another guest brings an appetizer without having first consulted the host(ess). During the conversation around the table, people discover that one of the guests is an accomplished singer. After the meal someone (not the hostess) encourages him to sing. After a song or two, someone asks what other hidden talents might be found among the guests. Eventually someone reveals that she does a few card tricks, and the group encourages the host(ess) to find a deck of cards. The cards remind another guest of a game. And so the evening goes. The host(ess) simply initiated the plans for the evening and made people feel welcome.

A similar contrast may be seen between programmatic and event-centered practices in the ordering of congregational ministries. We could look at the way congregations prepare for worship or study, or engage in mission in their communities. A conversation with the pastor of Oakhurst about how the congregation developed the financial support for its budget made the contrast clear for me. He told me that when he first came to the church, the congregation tried to follow what I am calling a programmatic process to shape its stewardship efforts. The denomination recommended an approach that had worked well in many churches. It involved a clear set of steps ranging from the establishment of congregational goals, to the identification of financial needs, to the development of a strategy to publicize these goals and needs, to the solicitation of pledges from the membership. The finance committee had the responsibility of coordinating and guiding each step of the process. Oakhurst quickly discovered that this approach did not work as well as they expected. The pastor then described the way they now raise the funds that support their ministries.

The congregation, he noted, does have a pledge drive each fall—planned by elected officers and subscribed to primarily by middle-class members who tend to develop personal budgets and make long-range personal spending plans. The congregation does not put too much effort into the pledge drive—mostly a letter to all members that includes a pledge card and designates a Sunday for collecting cards.

Equally important as the pledge drive are several memorial funds instituted when it became obvious that some people simply did not respond to planned strategies for raising money. These memorial funds are not endowed. They are named funds with designated purposes to support specific ministries and building maintenance. When a fund runs out of money, an appeal is made for money to renew it. The occasion provides an opportunity to recall the contributions of the person memorialized through the fund and to support the values of a particular ministry.

The combination of these two approaches to fund raising still did not meet all the congregation's obligations, nor did it provide a way to be responsive to new calls for ministries. So the congregation has a third pool of funds—called the pastor's discretionary fund—which the pastor may use to respond to any need he deems worthy. It also is replenished with an appeal to the membership.

These three approaches to fund raising exist side by side. They were not developed through careful strategy planning. Different people in and outside the congregation's committees take responsibility for their promotion. The congregation never has long-range assurance that income and expenses will approximate each other. "Fund raising" occurs all year, but the focus shifts from striving to meet budgets to stories about people who contributed significantly to the congregation and to projects that engage the congregation's imagination and commitment. Different strategies, different responses, order the funding of its ministries. When it tried to emphasize one of the three strategies over another, available funds inevitably declined.

Why does the congregation approach the funding of ministry in diverse ways? One answer has to do with differences in understandings about the meaning and function of money held by different groups. Middle-class folk—both black and white—work with long-range planning in their giving. Some members grew up in congregations and cultures in which the funding of ministries was based on personal appeals to specific programs and projects. They do not give money to a general budget. Still others, especially those with limited resources, can respond only when they have a little money on hand. Their resources are so limited that they cannot plan ahead. In fact, to confine the official and public strategy for funding church ministries to a pledge drive only reinforces their sense of margination in the congregation and community.

Fund raising at Oakhurst cannot be easily controlled or structured by a central committee or person. The various elements require different kinds of planning, involving different people in leadership. For the pastor, efforts to promote the interdependence of the people who give leadership to these different ways of raising funds is often like the experience of a juggler keeping several balls in the air at the same time. And yet, as leaders in the congregation have learned how to "juggle" their various ways of fund raising, they have discovered a coherence and purposefulness—indeed a design—that governs their efforts. Where some might see the presence of these diverse approaches to the funding of congregational life as fraught with tension and conflict, Oakhurst's pastor and most church members simply view it as the reality of the situation. It is not so much a problem as it is a catalyst to new possibilities.

Locating the Meaning of Time in the Fullness of a Moment

Event-centered practices for ordering congregational life tend to locate the meaning of time in the fullness of any given moment more than in the sequential movement of time from moment to moment. This may be especially characteristic of the multicultural congregation, perhaps because time is one of the most contested issues in the negotiations of its various cultural groups. There is rarely much discussion about when something should begin, but there is usually considerable difference in when people arrive for that planned activity or event. After a while each congregation develops a pattern to accommodate the various perspectives on time to be found among its members.

More important, the significance of a beginning and ending time diminishes as people increasingly focus attention on their experience of the time they meet together. In this regard time is highly relational in its content. Its meaning is intensified as their sense of solidarity increases. Victor Turner, who has studied the significance of rituals, called these moments of solidarity *communitas*. By this he meant that they have a liminal quality, blending "lowliness and sacredness," "homogeneity and comradeship." They are experienced as moments "in and out of time" as well as "in and out" of secular social structures. They reveal social bonds that lie beneath those of race, social class, gender, age, and education.[8] They establish relationships across the boundaries of race and culture. They point to possibilities for human relationships that do not typically occur in the routines of daily living. Perhaps it is no accident that these moments often occur ritually—as when the people of many nations at Northwoods hold hands to proclaim together that God is *"Our* Father," or when the Oakhurst congregation circles the sanctuary to sing fervently that a "sweet sweet spirit" exists in that place.

In programmatic strategies, time establishes boundaries for the exercise of programmatic interests. Designated beginning and ending times function as frames for experience and establish a rhythmic pattern of beginnings and endings.

Noting this, we may begin to discern the significant theological differences between event-centered and programmatic approaches to ordering congregational life. Theologically an event embodies eschatological memory. When a congregation orders its life around some event that links people with the common and disparate traditions and stories from the past even as it creates a vision for its future, it lives into the fullness of that possibility in the present moment. It emphasizes the identification of the community with the unfolding of the meanings and practices associated with these events. So the movement through the events of Lent and Easter, for example, is multilayered. It involves (1) the basic reenactment of the story—often in its various cultural forms—for communal remembering; (2) the living out of the story—enhanced by its multiple cultural perspectives—to embody its possibilities in the present; and (3) the envisioning of a future for the community—one that embraces the diversity of its experiences—through its rehearsal. People do not participate in the events of Lent and Easter so much to observe or hear again that ancient story, but to participate in it as it unfolds into the present experience of people. As such, event-centered practices emphasize the interplay of historical, contemporary, and future aspects of community.

When congregations embrace racial and cultural diversity, they can no longer assume that the past shared experience of community will continue into the future. The disruptive character of diversity confronts them with the recognition that community life is always fragile and needs to be intentionally sustained and renewed. And yet in the embracing of diversity, they also discover that it functions as a catalyst to new possibilities in community life. Indeed some people in these congregations refer to their encounters with difference as being the work of the Holy Spirit. God is at work through them creating something new. The power of the experience of that moment, in other words, takes precedence in the ordering of congregational life over the routines and structures of scheduled time.

For Further Reflection

An Exercise

Directions:
This exercise is a guide for exploring the extent to which the dynamics of an event-centered approach are present in some activity or event in the ministry of your congregation.

1. Choose an activity or ministry occasion that involved something of a

cross-section of the people in the congregation. It could be the weekly gathering of the congregation for worship.

2. Identify all the people who had designated responsibilities for this activity or ministry and the tasks they fulfilled in preparing for it.

3. Identify any people or groups who helped prepare for or fulfilled some role in the activity or ministry who had not been asked to do so.

4. Identify any person or group who gave leadership to some action that supported and reinforced the intent of this activity or ministry. For example, a Sunday school class that provides volunteer help in the nursery, contributes money to support some aspect of the activity, or organizes its monthly fellowship dinner around the theme of the activity.

5. Through what official channels did people hear about this activity or ministry? Through what unofficial channels did people also hear about it?

6. What did people contribute to the activity or ministry that the planning committee did not anticipate or, in some cases, even know about until after it happened?

7. As you ponder the answers to these questions, discuss among yourselves: In what ways did the unexpected and unplanned elements of this activity enhance or detract from people's participation in it?

8. In a final step, explore to what extent event-centered practices order the ministries of your congregation.

CHAPTER 6

Leadership in Multicultural Congregations

Up to this point our discussion of leadership has been relatively implicit. I have identified some of the distinctive things leaders in multicultural congregations do, the approaches they take to the multiple perspectives they encounter in the constituencies of their congregations, and ways they relate to the institutions or organizations through which they minister. But we have not discussed leadership as such. In this final chapter, that is our task. In one of the more interesting recent books on leadership, Howard Gardner begins with a rather common view of leadership: the capacity to "influence the thoughts, behaviors, and/or feelings of others." Richard Bondi notes that this influence involves moving people through time and through the changes that take place in relationships and institutions. He defines Christian leadership as those influences directed to "helping Christian communities embody the presence of Christ in the world today, so that we truly reflect the character of the God we profess." Both men locate the dynamics of leadership in the storytelling of communities. Gardner observes that some tell or relate the stories integral to the life and mission of communities. We see this in the preaching and teaching of pastors and Sunday school and Bible teachers, in the supervision of dramatic productions of Christmas and Easter. But leaders also convey the stories of the community in indirect ways—through their writing, their artistic expression, their embodiment of the values integral to the stories.[1]

Gardner identifies three kinds of leaders. Rare are the *visionary* leaders who occasionally make their mark on history. They are distinguished by their capacity to envision bold new possibilities for communities. Examples range from Moses, Jesus, and Mohammed to the contemporary Gandhi, Mother Teresa, and Martin Luther King, Jr. Most common are the *ordinary* leaders who "simply relate the traditional story of their group as effectively as possible." They do not stretch the consciousness of the group through their leadership, but they do reveal the commonplace stories that inform and shape the group or community's life together—an important task for any community seeking to maintain its identity, values, and institutions into the future. *Innovative* leaders, by way of contrast, take "a story that has been latent" in the group or community and bring to it "new attention or a fresh twist." The genius of innovative leaders exists in the capacity to identify stories and themes in a community's heritage that have been "muted or neglected" over the years, perhaps centuries. They bring them to the foreground of people's consciousness as a resource to the renewal and transformation of the life of the community. [2]

Among the leaders of multicultural congregations we have visited, we saw what seemed to be an unusual ability to draw on the strengths of these three patterns of leadership. Their commitment is sustained and imaginations for community life are fired by the visionary leadership of Moses, Jesus, Paul, and certain saints of the church, past and present. The need to tell culturally specific stories of Christian identity and vocation—the ordinary stories—over and over again in the quest for a common vocabulary of faith energizes their preaching and teaching. The overlap of cultural traditions and practices with centuries of painful and often violent cross-racial/cultural encounters calls forth from them an innovative spirit directed to the embodiment of a vision of community that embraces the diversity of God's creation. The interplay of these three patterns of leadership provides a framework for exploring several characteristics we discovered in the patterns of leadership among the clergy and laity of multicultural congregations.

Transformative Leadership

The leadership of multicultural congregations is transformative. Primary attention is not given to maintaining the status quo of any one group but to the nurture of change in the congregation for the sake of a new relationship among racially and culturally diverse groups and ultimately with God. In the three congregations we described in *We Are the Church Together*, transformation gained impetus with the arrival of new pastors.

At Cedar Grove the pastor took a statement this all-white congregation had used to define itself—the Cedar Grove family—and reinterpreted the meaning of *family* so as to cross racial boundaries. "Brother" and "sister" now transcend kin and race. At Oakhurst the transformation of congregational identity began when the pastor, drawing on the Pauline images of the interdependence of the members of the body of Christ, seized control of the decisions about who did and did not have power in the congregation and then redistributed it in a more equitable and inclusive manner. At Northwoods the transformation began with the new pastor's first sermon, which shifted the location of the eschatological vision of Revelation 7 from the distant future to the immediate present in that community. The actions of these pastors originated in their relationships to previously unemphasized or "lost" visionary themes in the historic story of Christian community. Their leadership took root as people began to hear and respond to new possibilities for their congregations in the stories they were relating.

The transformation of these congregations, however, did not occur only through the efforts of their clergy and other staff. A member from Cedar Grove suggested that it required stubborn laypeople who caught the pastor's vision and stayed with the congregation through its struggle to reenvision itself. We found his comment quite insightful. Being stubborn meant having enough commitment to a given community to give up "things as they are" to embrace what might be. Because the future would not be the same as the past, being stubborn also meant that the vision of what might be had to be powerful enough to sustain the congregation through fears experienced in the midst of often radical changes. The ability to face, even embrace, these fears—from the fear of the loss of the familiar, to the fear of demands from unknown others, to the fear of ridicule from old friends and neighbors who do not share the vision of a new kind of congregation, to the fear of not having much control over the congregation's future, to the fear of pain in unlearning old ways of cross-cultural and -racial relating—is a major feature in the pastoral and key lay leadership of multicultural congregations.

I have already described how the multicultural congregation may both transmit and hand on cultural traditions of its various constituencies and transform those traditions in a process of mutual appreciation and critique. I am increasingly convinced that the ability to face the fear of change has its roots in this leadership dynamic. The encounter with otherness brings to consciousness the importance of cultural traditions and practices. We become interested in who we are when we discover someone who is different from us. This storytelling capacity integral to "ordinary leadership" renews and reinforces the identification of people with their own respective heritages. At the same time the encounter with otherness brings to the surface the dehumanizing and oppressive features in our various cultural traditions and practices. Through mutual critique diverse racial and cultural groups confront each other with the necessity of significantly changing their relationships if they are to live redemptively with each other. This is a feature of innovative leadership.

Leadership in the multicultural congregation must necessarily embrace both dynamics. In the renewal of cultural identity, transformative leaders extend into the future people's respective cultures. In the transformation of those cultural traditions, they help create new possibilities for living into human community. The one dynamic reinforces the congregation's connection to the steadfastness of God's love for people in their particular cultures. The other enlivens its sense of God's presence in the re-creation of community. Both emphases in transformative leadership counter the fear of change people experience when they encounter difference.

Anticipatory Leadership

The leadership of multicultural congregations is also anticipatory. This is not a word I have found in the literature on leadership, but I have discovered no other that adequately captures this important aspect of innovative leadership in multicultural congregations. Anticipatory leadership is something akin to proactive leadership, in which leaders anticipate questions that might be asked, issues that might be posed, and problems that might occur, and they prepare possible responses. The opposite is a reactive leader who waits until something happens and then makes decisions based upon what is previously known. Groups can grow and change with either kind of leadership.

But my use of the word *anticipatory* goes beyond the capacity to discern optional courses of action for any plan. Anticipatory leaders as a matter of course see a situation or event from the future rather than from the past. They rarely ask questions about how things have been done (even though they may have a keen historical consciousness); instead they usually ask about how things might be done. It is an eschatological perspective—one that begins with the memory of the vision a group or community holds for its future more than with the memory of its history.

This is a critical capacity for leaders in multicultural congregations. They have few precedents to guide their efforts. The only stories in the Christian tradition about congregations embracing differences exist on the edges of our storytelling. Certainly we have rehearsed Paul's famous dictum that in Christ there shall be no Greek or Jew, male or female. But that has rarely been seen as an affirmation of the Jewishness of Jewish Christians and the Greekness of Greek Christians. Rather, it has been interpreted as a preferred state that exists beyond our particular religious and cultural heritages. So when the pastor of Northwoods posed the possibility of becoming a multicultural congregation, he in fact did not know from his past experience what he was talking about. And yet he did know, for he drew on a visionary story in the New Testament depicting a community of people from all the tribes and nations of the world gathered together and bound in fellowship by their relationship to Jesus Christ. What that would look like in the worship, education, administration, and mission of the Northwoods Church was not explained in the biblical text. The implications of that vision would have to be worked out in each worship service, each mission activity, each Bible study class, each committee meeting.

Relational Leadership

In multicultural congregations, leadership emphasizes relationality in establishing ground rules for corporate conduct and decision making. A pertinent point for leaders in multicultural congregations has been made by Sharon Welch: "The idea that there is a common interest, shared by all, reached by transcending our special interests, is fundamentally ideological." The point is that ideology is ultimately divisive—as is evident in Bosnia, the Near East, and in the political arguments over social issues in church and public life in this country. It sets the advocates of one perspective or point of view over against another. Welch continues that, given our "past and extant systems of exclusion and oppression, the experiences and even the needs of different groups of people are radically diverse."[3] Black and white children who participate in the same Sunday school class do not come with minds empty as blank slates, as teachers still living in the shadow of John Locke's psychological theories often assume. Instead, students engage one another, the teacher, and the subject matter even as they remain embedded in structures shaped by centuries of white privilege and black oppression. They may cope with that reality in a variety of ways. But the teacher of that class who ignores that reality perpetuates it.

An African-American mother in one of my classes made the case clearly. She discovered after several weeks that her five-year-old spent a considerable amount of time in a disciplinary corner in a church-sponsored, progressive, preschool program. During a consultation with the school director, a psychologist, and the classroom teacher, it became clear that the behavior of this child was not out of the ordinary. But being the only black child in the class meant that his behavior was more visible to the white teachers than that of other children. Unconsciously teachers espousing progressive and inclusive notions of education were reproducing a pattern of oppression and subjugation of this child.

The persistence of ancient patterns of relating contributes to our tendency to notice people with handicapping conditions; to see a woman in a place we would traditionally expect to see a man; to notice people of Korean or Finnish descent in a place traditionally associated with people of African descent; or to see and hear the restless movements of children if we expect behavior associated with adults in worship.

Similar issues face the pastor and the lay leadership of a culturally and racially diverse congregation. Centuries of embedded patterns of interrelating challenge the adequacy of any institutional structure to promote the solidarity envisioned in Paul's image of the church as the body of Christ. Those structures all too often only perpetuate oppressive or paternalistic patterns of relating. As the pastor of Oakhurst learned, elections can be maneuvered by people of dominant groups that claim to be inclusive and yet hold on to their control of resources and the content of congregational ministries.

As leaders in culturally and racially diverse congregations encounter these inhibiting dynamics in their structures and practices, they seek ways to enhance the quality of the relationships among diverse groups. This feature of multicultural congregations has already been described in the chapters on relational ties and conversation. The ultimate goal is not empathic leadership in which leaders intentionally seek to understand and "share" the "perceptions, thoughts, feelings," even the "muscular tensions," of others. Although empathy is a value of leadership in any group, among racially and culturally diverse groups it is also often impossible. The differences in background and perception are often too deep and profound to be shared. Indeed it is presumptuous for men to say they "feel" what a woman feels in childbirth or that Mexican Americans can perceive the order of the universe in quite the same way that a Chinese American can or that people with privileged economic status can understand the world of those who may have lost—even temporarily—all efforts to maintain some economic viability.

David Augsberger describes a characteristic of relationality that is often found in the leadership of culturally diverse congregations. It involves the capacity to bracket one's own cultural assumptions and perspectives so as to "enter the other's world of assumptions, beliefs, and values and temporarily take them as one's own." I have previously described this process as one of momentarily suspending one's own cultural values and perspectives to embrace the possibilities in a sister or brother. Here one attempts to envision "what the other believes, see as the other sees, value what the other values, and feel the consequent feelings as the other feels them." From this perspective leaders do not make assumptions about what people perceive, think, feel, and value. They are intensely conscious of the gulf that exists between themselves and those with whom they work. And the presence of that gulf requires them to learn how to see and to understand as the other sees and understands.[4]

Temporarily suspending one's cultural perspectives and practices is not foreign to our experience. I think of children whose eyes fill with wonder when they see the baby Jesus in the manger during a Christmas pageant. They know the baby is a doll, yet they also see the infant *Jesus* in the manger. I think of my decisions to suspend my own taste in foods to enjoy the feast set before me by new friends in another culture and place. I think of the decisions of the people in each congregation we studied to suspend their "time" preferences as they together entered into an event of worship, fellowship, or mission. When the moment is over, people return to their own ways of seeing, thinking, and doing—and yet they can never return to those patterns without the consciousness of the experience they had in relationship with someone who saw, thought, and did things somewhat differently. As I have mentioned before, the most powerful moments in these times of solidarity are typically identified with the indwelling presence of God. In the most intimate of encounters with the otherness of some person or group, in other words, those who embrace that otherness similarly have a sense of the significance of their relationship with the source of their respective differences. Perhaps this is what it means to "love God" most fully when we love our neighbors as ourselves.

The dynamics of relationality in leadership are typically found in the organization of a potluck supper more than in a committee meeting. At Northwoods, they can be seen in the planning and conduct of worship. The pastor, like a good chef, choreographs the contributions of the various people and groups giving leadership to worship. Yet, as we have already noticed, the choir prepares its work. The ushers order the sanctuary. The women in charge of the acolytes rehearse the young people who will assume those responsibilities. If children are reading one of the scripture lessons, the teachers help them practice. Some people bring flowers. Others may hang banners. A couple of the trustees check the thermostats and often end up doing some last-minute repair work on an aging heating and air conditioning system. When the liturgy begins, the pastor gives announcements for the week. Then the minister of youth, the choir director, and various laypeople with assigned roles take over until it is time for the pastor to preach—that is unless he has asked one of the seminary students or a lay leader to do so. He is involved, but he has little control over all that happens.

Leadership and Power

In multicultural congregations the embracing of differences heightens the leaders' awareness of the power dynamics in the encounter of diverse groups. A recent experience in the Sunday school class I help teach may illustrate several such power issues. The class currently has an enrollment of eighteen children, although attendance may range from nine on low Sundays to twenty when cousins and grandchildren are visiting. A slight majority of the children were born in Liberia or in the United States of Liberian parents. Several of their families have temporary-status visas, which means that when the State Department deems Liberia a safe place to live, they will be expected to leave or will be deported. Several children are European American. One family is Korean American. In the recent past the group has also included children of Peruvian, Nigerian, and African-American ancestry. My coteacher, from Liberia, is a former school principal. She and I are constantly confronted with a range of issues, emerging from our relationship as teachers to each other, to the children we teach, to the various cultures represented among the children and their families, to our relationship to the congregation and its ministries, and to the ways we respond to the larger public circumstances that affect the lives of all of us in that classroom.

Some of these issues are the typical dynamics of power that occur in any educational setting with children—who gets to speak and act; how boundaries are set and affirmation is distributed; how learning opportunities are constructed and learning is recognized. These issues have to do with the way my colleague and I respond to the interplay of gender, and of cultural, racial, and class attitudes and actions the children bring to our time together. The cultural content of the pictures we put on the wall, the patterns of turn taking we establish, the stories we tell, and the ways we interpret our biblical and theological traditions all reveal the extent of our sensitivity to the ways we exercise the power we have as leaders/teachers.

Not so typical are several social, political, economic, and religious issues that accompany the children into the classroom each time we meet. So we find ourselves in the middle of conversations between one child, secure in a solidly middle-class home of U.S. citizens, and another U.S.-born child (a U.S. citizen) whose financially strapped single mother struggles against language and cultural barriers to good employment while not knowing when her visa status might change, possibly forcing her to return to a war-ravaged land. And these two children then relate to a third child, whose immigrant parents are deeply committed to his education, but whose hard work at low wages leaves them little time to support the child in his studies. Other children present us with still other issues about how we as teachers communicate the gospel in ways that might contribute to their well-being as children of God. These issues seem a little academic until one discovers that the child who acts up in class did not have any breakfast that morning, or that an unusually reticent child has become aware of the violent death of a family member in a far away country, or that an angry child may only be acting out the frustrations of being in an overcrowded school with overworked teachers trying to respond to children speaking some twenty different languages.

Even more complex are the dynamics evident as we teachers, out of our own cultural contexts, respond to the words and actions of our students. I see that I typically emphasize helping people to discover and develop their gifts and talents. In the children I see unique gifts and possibilities that, with appropriate support and guidance, should help them become faithful disciples and creative citizens of the world. While my Liberian colleague recognizes the value of this rather individualistic approach to teaching, she focuses on helping children learn to take on the values, norms, and expectations of the church or adult community into which they will grow. My values seek to help students develop their gifts to the best of their ability to enrich and enhance the life of the community. My colleague seeks to help students learn to be responsible and effective contributors to the community's common values and goals. Each Sunday morning the children we teach live in the midst of our own negotiations. We have come to embrace the importance of both her expectations and mine. The children we teach will be negotiating both sets of expectations as youth and adults in an increasingly pluralistic world. The challenge before us is to help them become conscious of the differences in our expectations of them. This consciousness of our different approaches may lead them to an ever-increasing awareness of the various cultural assumptions, values, and practices they experience in the church and school. A school teacher in the Cedar Grove congregation articulated the importance of that kind of consciousness. She reported that children from the Cedar Grove Church were the only children in the school where she taught who consistently moved comfortably back and forth between black students and teachers and white students and teachers. These children had learned how to live with and to negotiate the cultural differences of those two groups in church. They drew on those learnings in negotiating the racial and cultural dynamics of their school.

In this description of the power dynamics in the Sunday school class I teach, I see three implications for congregational leadership. First, the presence of diversity means that every leadership activity engages us in the power dynamics among the various racial and cultural groups. Our Sunday school class is not simply the setting in which we as teachers and students work out our individual perspectives on what is appropriate behavior, attitudes, or beliefs. Those perspectives are negotiated through the ways we engage each other in working through our common tasks. *Negotiation* is the key word here—in regard to the entire congregation.

That negotiation, however, needs to be governed by what Sharon Welch has called a "communicative ethic." And this brings me to the second implication, involving the persistent effort to create the conditions in which all parties have the freedom to recognize their concrete otherness, leading to the possibility of both mutual affirmation and critique. This is the dynamic of solidarity[5]—perhaps most poignantly envisioned in Martin Buber's description of the relationship of a wholly "I" and a wholly "Thou." Neither of us is an "it"; we engage each other as "partners," to use another image of solidarity, found in the writing of Letty Russell. We exist alongside each other—neither overwhelmed nor overwhelming, intimidated nor intimidating, controlled nor controlling—but interacting with the freedom of intimacy and the responsibility of mutual critique. In other words, we need the other to be more fully honest in our own particularity.

And this leads to our third implication and insight. There are no quick "ten steps" to the creation of multicultural congregations or the maintenance of their ministries. The congregations I visited that most fully celebrate the mutual give and take of the giftedness of their various cultural and racial constituencies have had long pastorates—six, eight, fifteen, twenty years. These pastors have typically stepped out of the career ladders of their denominations to embrace a new vision for congregational life. But it is not only long-term pastorates that have been instrumental. Each of these congregations has also had lay leaders who have shared the congregational vision of a distinctive community of difference, and these leaders have lived into that vision for many years. In many instances both pastors and laypeople have lost friends who did not understand their commitment to this new vision for congregational community. Rarely do these people receive much public recognition for the challenge of their efforts. And yet most would admit that their experience is similar to that of the excited pastor who, at the end of his third year in a particular pastorate, told me that things were just beginning to happen in the congregation. He could hardly wait to find out what the next year would bring. He told me the same thing when I saw him four or five years later and again several years later. When he retired—after the normal retirement age—he voiced his regret in leaving because "things are just starting to happen here." It is this sense of eschatological expectation that nurtures the spirituality that sustains a diverse community through years of negotiating its differences. It is a spirituality that anticipates the surprising work of the Holy Spirit in the midst of these negotiations. It is a spirituality that celebrates the deepening of relationships even as those involved discover ever more clearly how distinctively "other" they are to each other. For them, diversity is not a problem to be overcome; it is a gift to be celebrated.

For Further Reflection

Directions:
Return to the reflection exercise at the end of chapter 5. Consider the development of the event and the ordering of the congregation around that event. Identify where you saw examples of (1) ordinary leadership, (2) innovative leadership, and (3) the influence of the visionary leadership of significant people in the history of the church. Name specific people and groups and in a few words describe what they did. Then explore ways their leadership perspective and behavior contributed to (or inhibited) the congregation's preparation for participation in this event.

Examples of ordinary leadership:

Examples of innovative leadership:

Examples of the influence of visionary leaders from the past on the current leaders of this event:

NOTES

Introduction

1. A full account of the stories of these three congregations may be found in Charles Foster and Theodore Brelsford, *We Are the Church Together: Cultural Diversity in Congregational Life* (Valley Forge, PA: Trinity Press, 1996). Two questions informed our approach to the study of these congregations: How do culturally and racially diverse congregations understand themselves to be church? And how do they go about the task of incorporating children and newcomers into that understanding? The focus, in other words, was on the interplay of ecclesiology and education.

2. Although the literature on multiculturalism in general is vast and that on cultural diversity in the church is growing, four books stand out as important references for anyone interested in knowing more about leadership in culturally and racially diverse congregations: William Cenkner, *The Multicultural Church: A New Landscape in U.S. Theologies* (Mahwah, NJ: Paulist Press, 1996); Eric Lay, *The Wolf Shall Dwell with the Lamb: A Spirituality for Leadership in a Multicultural Community* (St. Louis: Chalice Press, 1993); Eric Law, *The Bush Was Blazing but Not Consumed* (St. Louis: Chalice Press, 1996); Nibs Stroupe and Inez Fleming, *While We Run This Race: Confronting the Power of Racism in a Southern Church* (Maryknoll: Orbis, 1995).

3. See Stroupe and Fleming, *While We Run This Race*, for the story of Oakhurst Church's explicit efforts to challenge racism.

4. The list of thoughtful books on leadership in the church is long. Examples of the range of approach and perspective include: Richard Bondi, *Leading God's People: Ethics for the Practice of Ministry* (Nashville, Abingdon Press, 1989); Letty M. Russell, *Church in the*

Round: Feminist Interpretation of the Church (Louisville: Westminster/ John Knox Press, 1993), ch. 2; Robert M. Schwartz, *Servant Leaders of the People of God: An Ecclesial Spirituality for American Priests* (Mahwah, NJ: Paulist Press, 1989); Loughlan Sofield, S.T., and Donald H. Kuhn, *The Collaborative Leaders: Listening to the Wisdom of God's People* (Notre Dame, IN: Ave Maria Press, 1995); Lovett H. Weems, Jr., *Church Leadership: Vision, Team, Culture, and Integrity* (Nashville, Abingdon Press, 1993); James D. Whitehead and Evelyn Eaton Whitehead, *Method in Ministry: Theological Reflection and Christian Ministry* (New York: Seabury Press, 1980).

5. Dorothy C. Bass, *Practicing Our Faith: A Way of Life for a Searching People* (San Francisco: Jossey-Bass, 1997), xi.

6. Clifford H. Geertz, *The Interpretation of Cultures* (New York: Basic Books, 1973), 216; C.A. Bowers and David J. Flinders, *Responsive Teaching: An Ecological Approach to Classroom Patterns of Language, Culture, and Thought* (New York: Teachers College Press, 1990), 18.

Chapter 1

1. Miroslav Volf, "God's Spirit and God's People in the Social and Cultural Upheavals in Europe," *Journal of Ecumenical Studies* 29, no. 2 (Spring, 1992): 230-48.

2. Eric Law, *The Wolf Shall Dwell with the Lamb: A Spirituality for Leadership in a Multicultural Community* (St. Louis: Chalice Press, 1993), 2-4. In a provocative discussion of the incompatibility of wolves and lambs in Isaiah's vision of the "peaceable realm," Law explores the dynamics at work in the leadership of multicultural communities. We will return to his discussion in Chapter 4.

3. The stories of culturally and racially diverse congregations may be found in all forms of media. The *Times-Union* of Jacksonville, Florida, for example, featured several congregations in its 7 July, 1996, "Insight" section. Henry G. Brinton, "Finding Room in God's House," *Washington Post*, 16 March 1997, C1-2, explores the impact of immigrants on U.S. churches; Sue M. Mote, "The Church of Many Colors," *Presbyterian Today*, October 1996, features the Oakhurst Church. Mote's article exemplifies the growing interest of denominational magazines in the experience of racially and culturally diverse congregations. Maya Angelou narrated the story of the Glide Memorial Church (San Francisco) for "Rainbow in the Clouds," a public television documentary.

4. Feminist, liberation, and black theologians and missiologists have contributed significantly to new understandings of the local church. Works that attend to issues of ecclesiology from a multicultural perspective include: Ruy O. Costa, ed., *One Faith, Many Cultures* (Maryknoll, NY: Orbis, 1982); Susan Brooks Thistlethwaite and Mary Potter Engel, eds., *Lift Every Voice: Constructing Christian Theologies from the Underside* (San Francisco: Harper & Row, 1990); Jung Young Lee, *Marginality: The Key to Multicultural Theology* (Minneapolis: Fortress Press, 1995).

5. *1992 Mission Yearbook for Prayer and Study* (Louisville: Presbyterian Church U.S.A. General Assembly Council, 1992).

6. Oakhurst Presbyterian Church (Atlanta, GA) Mission Statement.

7. M. Shawn Copeland, "Self-Identity in a Multicultural Church in a Multicultural Context," in *The Multicultural Church: A New Landscape in U.S. Theologies*, ed. William Cenkner (Mahwah, NJ: Paulist Press, 1996), 10.

8. Lawrence L. Cremin, *American Education: The National Experience 1783-1876* (New York: Harper Colophon Books, 1980), 245.

9. See for example, C. Peter Wagner, *Our Kind of People: The Ethical Dimensions of Church Growth in America* (Atlanta: John Knox Press, 1979); or the more recent James Breckenridge and Lillian Breckenridge, *What Color Is Your God? Multicultural Education in the Church* (Wheaton, IL: Victor/SP Publications, 1995).

10. John Koenig, *New Testament Hospitality: Partnership with Strangers as Promise and Mission* (Philadelphia: Fortress Press, 1985), 3.

11. A helpful discussion of the dynamics of immigration and diversity on the religious landscape of the nation may be found in E. Allen Richardson, *Strangers in This Land: Pluralism and the Response to Diversity in the United States* (New York: Pilgrim Press, 1988).

12. Law, *The Wolf Shall Dwell*, 3.

13. Ibid., 3ff.

14. Edward T. Hall, *The Silent Language* (Greenwich, CT: Fawcett, 1959), 39.

15. David A. Hollinger, *Postethnic America* (New York: Basic Books, 1995), x.

Chapter 2

1. See C. Ellis Nelson, *Congregations: Their Power to Form and Transform* (Atlanta: John Knox Press, 1988) 7-9; James F. Hopewell, *Congregations: Stories and Structures* (Philadelphia: Fortress Press, 1987), 13-14.

2. Robert J. Schreiter, *Constructing Local Theologies* (Maryknoll, NY: Orbis, 1986), 1-6, has drawn our attention, perhaps more than anyone, to the growing interest in theological discussions on the influence of local circumstances in shaping our responses to the gospel. He has called this emerging pattern of theological reflection "local theology," in part because it recognizes the constructive role of "local" churches in the theological enterprise.

3. Ibid., 1-3.

4. Sidney E. Mead, *The Lively Experiment: The Shaping of Christianity in America* (New York: Harper & Row, 1963), 104.

5. Wade Clark Roof and William McKinney, *American Mainline Religion: Its Changing Shape and Future* (New Brunswick, NJ: Rutgers University Press, 1987), 49-51.

6. Pentecostal congregations often espouse this perspective. Shared experience may be more important than racial or cultural heritage in the congregation. But many Pentecostal congregations, unlike those we are describing, do not necessarily embrace the racial and cultural diversity of their members as gifts for their minsitries.

7. See *Effective Christian Education: A National Study of Protestant Congregations* (Minneapolis: Search Institute, 1990), 23ff., for data on the shift of loyalty from denomination to congregation.

8. C. Peter Wagner, *Our Kind of People: The Ethical Dimensions of Church Growth in America* (Atlanta: John Knox Press, 1979), 14-16.

9. The lack of cultural consciousness of dominant-culture people is a primary critique in much of the literature on multiculturalism. Several denominations, for example, have offices of multicultural ministries that in fact oversee only those ministries of racial and ethnic minority groups. This is also the approach taken in James Breckenridge and Lillian Breckenridge, *What Color Is Your God: Multicultural Education in the Church* (Wheaton, IL: Victor/SP Publications, 1995).

10. Wagner, *Our Kind of People*, 4.

11. H. Richard Niebuhr, *Christ and Culture* (New York: Harper Torchbooks, 1951).

12. Schreiter, *Constructing Local Theologies*, 6-16.

13. G. Ronald Murphy, S.J., *The Saxon Savior: The Germanic Transformation of the Gospel in the Ninth-Century Heliand* (New York: Oxford University Press, 1989), ix, 4, 107.

14. A contemporary example might be M. Thomas Thangaraj, *The Crucified Guru: An Experiment in Cross-Cultural Christology* (Nashville: Abingdon Press, 1994).

15. Schreiter, *Constructing Local Theologies*, 13.

16. Letty M. Russell, *Household of Freedom: Authority in Feminist Theology* (Philadelphia: Westminster Press, 1987), 30.

17. See other examples of this approach to the study of the Bible in R. S. Sugirtharajah, ed., *Voices from the Margin: Interpreting the Bible in the Third World* (Maryknoll, NY: Orbis, 1991).

18. Fumitaka Matsuoka, "Pluralism at Home: Golobalization within North America," *Theological Education* 26 (Spring 1990) supplement I, 39-40.

19. For an extensive exploration of the dynamics of change in congregations and their communities, See Nancy Tatom Ammerman, *Congregation and Community* (New Brunswick, NJ: Rutgers University Press, 1997).

20. Signithia Fordham, "Racelessness as a Factor in Black Students' School Success: Pragmatic Strategy or Pyrrhic Victory?" in *Facing Racism in Education*, ed. Tamara Beauboeuf-Lafontant and D. Smith Augustine (Cambridge, MA: Harvard Educational Review, 196), Reprint Series 28, 213.

21. C.A. Bowers and David J. Flinders, *Responsive Teaching: An Ecological Approach to Classroom Patterns of Language, Culture, and Thought* (New York: Teachers College Press), 2.

22. See Sharon Welch, "An Ethic of Solidarity," in *Postmodernism, Feminism, and Cultural Politics: Redrawing Educational Boundaries*, ed. Henry A. Giroux (Albany: State University of New York Press, 1991), 83-99, for an expanded discussion of the ethic that underlies this description of a collaborative approach to multicultural power dynamics.

Chapter 3

1. John Koenig, *New Testament Hospitality: Partnership with Strangers as Promise and Mission* (Philadelphia: Fortress Press, 1985), 4-5.

2. Robert C. Worley, *A Gathering of Strangers: Understanding the Life of Your Church* (Philadelphia: Westminster Press, 1976).

3. Elliot Eisner, *The Educational Imagination* (New York: Macmillan, 1979), ch. 5, notes that curriculum contains three kinds of messages–explicit, implicit, and null–messages that are not explicitly present.

4. Chris Argyris, *Theory in Practice: Increasing Professional Effectiveness* (San Francisco: Jossey-Bass, 1974).

5. Henri J. M. Nouwen, *Reaching Out: The Three Movements of the Spiritual Life* (New York: Doubleday, 1975), 45, 55.

6. Sharon Welch, "An Ethic of Solidarity and Difference," in *Postmodernism, Feminism, and Cultural Politics: Redrawing Educational Boundaries*, ed. Henry A. Giroux (Albany: State University of New York Press, 1991), 95.

7. Walter Brueggemann, "The Legitimacy of a Sectarian Hermeneutic: 2 Kings 18-19," in *Education for Citizenship and Discipleship*, ed. Mary C. Boys (New York: Pilgrim Press, 1989), 3-34.

8. C. A. Bowers and David J. Flinders, *Responsive Teaching: An Ecological Approach to Classroom Patterns of Language, Culture, and Thought* (New York: Teachers College Press, 1990), 144-45.

9. Romney M. Moseley, David Jarvis, and James W. Fowler, *Manual for Faith Development Research* (Atlanta: Center for Faith Development, Candler School of Theology, Emory University, 1986), 18-24.

Chapter 4

1. Edward T. Hall, *The Silent Language* (Greenwich, CT: Fawcett, 1959), 46.

2. Charles R. Foster, "Communicating: Informal Conversation in the Congregation's Education," in *Congregations; Their Power to Form and Transform*, ed. C. Ellis Nelson (Atlanta: John Knox Press, 1988), 218-37.

3. C.A. Bowers and David J. Flinders, *Responsive Teaching: An Ecological Approach to Classroom Patterns of Language, Culture, and Thought* (New York: Teachers College Press, 1990), 102.

4. See Parker J. Palmer, *To Know as We Are Known: A Spirituality of Education* (San Francisco: Harper & Row, 1983), 69ff, for a thoughtful discussion on the relationship of space and freedom in the dynamics of teaching and learning.

5. Rebecca Chopp, *The Power to Speak: Feminism, Language, God* (New York: Crossroad, 1991), 2.

6. Bowers and Flinders, *Responsive Teaching*, 146-49.

7. Ibid., 146-47.

8. Eric Law, *The Wolf Shall Dwell with the Lamb: A Spirituality for Leadership in a Multicultural Community* (St. Louis: Chalice Press, 1993), 114-15.

9. Ibid., 102-103.

10. Robert Allen Warrior, "A Native American Perspective: Canaanites, Cowboys, and Indians," *Voices from the Margin: Interpreting the Bible in the Third World*, ed. R. S. Sugirtharajah (Maryknoll, NY: Orbis, 1991), 289.

11. David W. Augsberger, *Pastoral Counseling across Cultures* (Philadelphia: Westminster Press, 1986), 41.

Chapter 5

1. Lovett H. Weems, Jr., *Church Leadership: Vision, Team, Culture, and Integrity* (Nashville: Abingdon Press, 1993).

2. James F. White, *Introduction to Christian Worship* (Nashville: Abingdon Press, 1981), 23-24.

3. Perhaps it should be no surprise, in retrospect, that Letty Russell who was a member of the East Harlem Protestant Parish staff would later explore the dynamics of leadership through the metaphor of the table around which the community gathers to celebrate its life together and be nurtured for living out its faith in the world; see Letty Russell, *Church in the Round: Feminist Interpretation of the Church* (Louisville: Westminster/John Knox, 1993).

4. Larry Rasmussen, "Shaping Communities," in *Practicing Our Faith: A Way of Life for a Searching People*, ed. Dorothy C. Bass (San Francisco: Jossey-Bass, 1997), 119-20. Lovett Weems, in *Church Leadership*, uses the metaphor of dance to illustrate the role of leaders in the interplay of people and ministries in congregational life, page 118.

5. Charles Foster, *Educating Congregations: The Future of Christian Education* (Nashville: Abingdon Press, 1994), 29, 34ff.

6. Robert MacAfee Brown, *Is Faith Obsolete?* (Philadelphia: Westminster Press, 1974), 28ff.

7. See Lovett H. Weems, Jr., *Church Leadership: Vision, Team,*

Culture, and Integrity (Nashville: Abingdon Press, 1993), 41-45, for a helpful discussion of the characteristics of vision in leadership.

8. Victor Turner, *The Ritual Process: Structure and Anti-Structure* (Ithaca, NY: Cornell Paperbacks, 1969), 96.

Chapter 6

1. Howard Gardner, *Leading Minds: An Anatomy of Leadership* (New York: Basic Books, 1995), 5-6, 9; Richard Bondi, *Leading God's People: Ethics for the Practice of Ministry* (Nashville: Abingdon Press, 1989), 18.

2. Gardner, *Leading Minds*, 9-11.

3. Sharon Welch, "An Ethic of Solidarity and Difference," in *Postmodernism, Feminism, and Cultural Politics: Redrawing Educational Boundaries*, ed. Henry A. Giroux (Albany: State University of New York Press, 1991), 89.

4. David W. Augsberger, *Pastoral Counseling across Cultures* (Philadelphia: Westminster Press, 1986), 31-2.

5. Welch, "Ethic of Solidarity," 91.

92122

254.2
F754

254.2
F754

92122

LINCOLN CHRISTIAN COLLEGE AND SEMINARY

3 4711 00093 7807